BAKING

FOR

PLEASURE

BAKING

FOR

PLEASURE

COMFORTING RECIPES TO BRING YOU JOY

RAVNEET GILL

PAVILION

CONTENTS

A NOTE FROM RAV

I remember when my first book (*The Pastry Chef's Guide*) came out in 2020, I thought I'd release it and go about my day, maybe think about opening my own place eventually, but more importantly, I had a sense of relief and accomplishment because recipes of mine that I wanted to use regularly were now in an 'easy to carry around in my bag' sort of format. I received so many messages from chefs and other cooks in kitchens saying how much they enjoyed the handy, straightforward manner of the book, the pick-and-mix style of writing, and the less hand-holding and more practical elements of it.

Nathan Outlaw told his daughter that it would be the only book she would need if she wanted to start out as a pastry chef! Something I still can't quite believe. But I wrote it for that very purpose, to break down the fundamentals of pastry and give people the base recipes they needed that were reliable enough to eventually ease them into running their own section and creating desserts of their own.

'The intention of these recipes is to make them suitable for a home kitchen.'

Little did I know that, fast-forward three years, and I'd be writing this, my third book, after releasing my second book in 2021 (*Sugar, I Love You*)! Or that I would have the opportunities I am fortunate to have in front of me now, and be married, too, in a home that I own with a cat of my own, finally.

This is the book I couldn't have written had I still been working full-time in kitchens. It's a book full of recipes that I've been able to create because, for the first time since I started cooking professionally, I can take a moment to do it for pure pleasure, without the haste of service or catering for customers. Instead it's for enjoyment, for surprising friends and for eating with loved ones, or alone on the sofa.

During my time in professional kitchens, I was so absorbed by and totally engulfed in the lifestyle that often I had very little energy or time to cook or bake the things I enjoyed on my days off. Instead I'd opt for a take-away or to eat out.

My husband, Mattie, who I met working in a restaurant, still works full-time as a chef and his influence on me and my style of cooking, baking and eating is unparalleled. We are both big lovers of eating and find ourselves chatting about how a dish 'eats'. How it feels, texturally, what it could be and how to get it there. The two of us love hosting, and although the process is usually full of minor kitchen disputes, we create very fun dinners together. We will debate the menu for days, with Mattie focusing on the main course, while I take care of the starter and the dessert (plus the cleaning up!). His passion and knowledge of food makes me a better chef, and as I tested recipes for this book, Mattie was a massive part of making me not second-guess myself and he helped to push my ideas into creating desserts and dishes that have evolved into what we both find delicious.

I hope you will see the joy and love that is within these pages and find recipes that become your own. I also hope that it gives you the space to spend some time doing nice things and putting on spreads for the ones you love.

The intention of these recipes is to make them suitable for a home kitchen. I've had to be mindful of the washing up (!), being more resourceful with the amount of ingredients I use, and focusing on one recipe at a time and how it can work around an individual's schedule.

Rav x

'I always advocate for you to use my recipes as a base to create something of your own.'

FINDING JOY IN THE KITCHEN

HOME-BAKING

I don't know about you, but things tend to turn out a lot better in the kitchen when I'm on my own, with some music on and no outside distractions! I know this is rare and often not easy to do, but when it's my first time making something, I really love doing it alone and I think it makes a huge difference. Getting to grips with something unfamiliar when it's just you means you can focus on it and give it enough of your attention. I have made countless silly mistakes when I'm trying to do too many things at the same time, or when I think I know something like the back of my hand and get comfortable – those disasters always feel harder to get over.

If you want to regularly bake at home, I suggest making it easier for yourself by getting proper containers for the ingredients that you will use the most. This will make it easier for both storage and usage. Not only that, once they are clearly labelled and visible in your cupboard, it will save you from running to the shops to gather ingredients you already have. Making the process easier, from keeping all your baking tins in the same place to clearly storing your ingredients, will make baking enjoyable and a lot less stressful.

When you're baking or cooking something, start by thinking about how it's going to 'eat'. This will set you up to get properly in the zone to create something special. You'll know (if you've read my other books) that I always advocate for you to use my recipes as a base to create something of your own. It might be that you use one of the cake recipes as part of a plated dessert or a layered cake, you might want to change the flavoured butter in the cardamom or saffron buns and use another spice, for example, or adjust the mighty pavlova to suit the season, and so on. This is what it's all about.

'When you're baking or cooking something, start by thinking about how it's going to 'eat'.'

EQUIPMENT

When it comes to baking, it's really important to get to know your oven and to understand the impact it will have on the final result. All of the recipes in this book were tested using my home electric fan oven, which is very reliable with an even heat distribution throughout. This doesn't mean the recipes won't work in less reliable ovens, but if your oven can be a bit temperamental, please check the signs of what stage the recipe should be at. For example, if the instructions say to bake for 30 minutes or until the edges are golden brown, if at 30 minutes the edges are still pale, bake until the edges are golden. Keep looking for the signs, as this will improve your results and help you to become an even better baker with instinctual knowledge.

The majority of these recipes utilize a rotation of the same basic tin sizes, which I have found are widely available in most supermarkets in the baking section. If you find yourself stuck without the appropriate vessel to make or bake a dessert in, for example, if you have a smaller tin than you need, then the rule is simple. If baking a cake batter, fill the tin with batter until it reaches three-quarters of the way up the tin. Do not be tempted to overfill a tin, and remember to monitor the baking time if you are changing the tin size. Look for the signs!

A good stand mixer will always be very well used if you are someone who likes to bake often. It's a useful investment to make and can help you to create more advanced bakes. Although it's really nice to have one, it's also not essential. If you prefer an electric handheld whisk, use it to create volume when whipping or whisking and to cream together butter and sugar when making a cake batter. If you're not too familiar with handling dough, a stand mixer can work wonders for creating reliably consistent doughs. You can also make various doughs by hand, but it will require a bit more shoulder strength and resilience! The base doughs for things like puff pastry and the tarts in this book can easily be made using your hands, too.

I find it really helpful to have more than one handheld whisk and multiple spatulas in my drawer, a good sturdy rolling pin, saucepans and different-sized bowls for mixing. One of my laziest hacks is to buy pre-cut circles or squares of baking paper for lining my cake tins, which is a job I find very dull.

Some of these recipes require a blender for emulsifying or bringing things together – a standard blender works well and sometimes a stick blender does, too. I also use a food processor in some recipes.

I recommend a sturdy set of digital scales and standard teaspoon and tablespoon measures (or ideally, a set of measuring spoons). Buying the batteries for the scales is something I always forget, so now I buy a few and keep them in a box in my baking cupboard.

My last tip is to stock up on Tupperware or similar storage containers and be prepared to lose a few along the way after you send your guests home with slices or scoops of a dessert or bake.

KEY INGREDIENTS
AND COOKING NOTES

I've made sure that 95 per cent of the ingredients used in this book can be found easily in most local or larger supermarkets. This has also made my last-minute runs to the shops much easier – especially when re-testing recipes! It means that if you find yourself in the mood to bake, you should be able to get going pretty quickly once you've got everything you need.

A cliché thing to say, but it's true, is to buy the best ingredients you can afford. That goes for flour and sugar as much as it does for dairy and eggs. For example, when buying chocolate, I like to buy mine in the chocolate-bar aisle as opposed to the baking aisle – if a 70 per cent dark chocolate is needed, I find that a good-quality one I enjoy eating is the one I will also use for baking.

I like to buy golden caster sugar for baking, although regular caster sugar works really well, too. In the US, granulated sugar is more commonly used and it can work in these recipes. However, I sometimes find that it can lead to a more coarse result in some recipes as the sugar doesn't break down in the same way.

I mostly use unsalted butter, full-fat milk and double cream as the default dairy in this book. Whipping cream can be substituted for the double cream, if needed.

The eggs used throughout are UK medium (US large), approx. 50g each, unless otherwise specified.

When you are using yeast, the majority of recipes in this book utilize fast-action dried yeast, and I prefer to buy the sachets as opposed to a tin. I find that this ensures the yeast stays sealed and lasts for longer.

Fresh herbs have been used in all instances unless otherwise specified. When a recipe calls for grated zest of citrus fruit, buy unwaxed fruit and wash well before using.

I always recommend using metric measurements for precision when baking but have included tablespoon and teaspoon measurements at times for easier home-baking. You can find metric-imperial conversion charts on page 244 if you need, though it is important to work with only one set of measurements and not alternate between the two within a recipe.

Recipes have been tested in a fan oven, but non-fan/conventional electric and gas conversions are also included. Recipes have been tested using a microwave on medium power unless stated otherwise.

Though clingfilm is required at times in this book to keep food items fresh/wrapped, I also encourage the use of more eco-friendly alternatives (such as beeswax wraps, baking paper, lids, etc) wherever possible.

BREAD-MAKING

Moving into bread territory now, I want to take you through a few different ways of making various breads. From focaccia to Japanese milk loaf and flatbreads. Bread-making is not something that should be feared or put into the corner, it's actually incredibly forgiving if you get a feel for the signs you're looking for. Pay attention to touch, feel, appearance and smell, as judging when it's ready is all in those beautiful changes and details.

In principle, here are a few useful tips to note for the bread recipes in this book, before you get started:

Yeast and salt shouldn't touch directly.

When adding water to a dough, it shouldn't be anywhere near scalding hot, it should be tepid or hand-hot and feel pleasant – judge it by dipping your finger in (it shouldn't feel ice-cold but it also shouldn't feel too hot that it startles you; if you're not sure, stay on the colder side, as it's better to be colder than too warm – if it's too hot, it will kill the yeast).

After the initial mix, the dough should be left to rise/prove either above room temperature in a warm place or in the fridge (it will take longer in the fridge). It should rise up with air bubbles. If it doesn't rise properly then the yeast might be too old and inactive, so you will need to start again.

After shaping, the dough can also be placed in the fridge overnight for a slow prove. It will then need to be brought back to room temperature before baking. Take it out of the fridge for a few hours until it's soft and looks puffy (as it would have looked had it not been in the fridge overnight).

After degassing the dough (also known as 'knocking back'), which I tend to do by folding the dough over on itself several times, it will deflate and need a second rise/prove after shaping.

You can use a dusting of flour when shaping the doughs in this book, but use it sparingly and have a dough scraper to hand to help where needed.

A dough scraper is really good for helping to get the dough off your hands, bowls and surfaces and also to help shape doughs.

Before baking, ensure the oven is pre-heated properly.

'Pay attention to
touch, feel, appearance
and smell.'

PASTRY-MAKING

The pastry recipes in this book can be made by hand, in a food processor or in a stand mixer. When you are making pastry, it's important to handle it correctly and to not overwork it. Remember, pastry's best friend is the fridge! If it ever gets too difficult to handle, pop it on a tray and place it in the fridge to chill out for a bit.

Making pastry by hand is extremely rewarding and after a little practise becomes very easy.

I'm also aware that a lot of people like to buy ready-made pastry – this is ok! If it makes you feel more comfortable or if time is not on your side, there are some great ready-made pastry options (chilled fresh and frozen varieties) available in a lot of supermarkets.

If you do want a quick reference to a classic puff pastry, here is my go-to recipe...

Recipe overleaf →

'Remember,
pastry's best friend
is the fridge!'

CLASSIC PUFF PASTRY

MAKES 2.5KG

1kg strong white flour, plus extra
   for dusting

15g fine sea salt

250g cold unsalted butter, cubed

450ml water

25ml white wine vinegar (this helps
   prevent the formation of gluten)

750g unsalted butter, cut into large pieces

This classic full puff pastry recipe uses 'the single turn method' (also known as a 'letter fold'). This is where you fold the piece of dough into three. Classic puff pastry requires a total of six single turns. The benefit of making six single turns is that you will end up with lots of layers and a really delicate puff.

1. First make the dough. Place the flour and salt in a mixing bowl and rub the butter in using your fingertips until the butter is incorporated and invisible. You can also do this using the paddle attachment in a stand mixer if you prefer.

2. Mix together the water and white wine vinegar in a separate bowl, then pour into the bowl and mix until a dough forms. Do not over-mix. Wrap the dough in clingfilm and rest in the fridge for at least 2 hours.

3. Prepare the butter by pounding it into the size of roughly an A5 sheet of paper between two large sheets of baking paper with a rolling pin. Wrap in clingfilm and chill in the fridge for at least 2 hours (or until it's the same temperature as the chilled dough).

4. Now you need to laminate the butter into the dough. Dust the work surface lightly with flour. With a short side nearest to you, gently roll out the dough vertically until it's only slightly longer than a sheet of A4 paper. Place the butter on the bottom two-thirds of the dough. Fold the top third of the dough down over half of the butter and then fold the bottom third (with the rest of the butter on it) up over the first fold. Turn the dough 90 degrees to the right. This is called a 'single turn'.

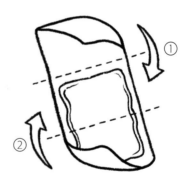

5. Roll the dough (with the butter in it) vertically again to the same size as before and about 1cm (⅜in) thick. (Try to roll in one direction only to prevent widening your strip of dough, you only want to elongate it. Flour the rolling pin and work surface and turn the dough over from time to time if you need to stop it from sticking). Then, fold the top third down and the bottom third up and over the first third once again. Turn by 90 degrees, and repeat again. Cover and rest in the fridge for 2 hours.

6. Take the pastry out of the fridge 15 minutes before you plan to work with it again. Rotate the puff pastry a quarter clockwise after resting and before rolling out again. It should look like a book you can open out before you begin rolling. Repeat the same process as step 5 to make two more single turns (letter folds), and then wrap and rest the pastry in the fridge again for another 2 hours.

7. Make two final single turns (following step 5 twice), then wrap and rest in the fridge again for a minimum of 2 hours before using. You should have made six single turns (letter folds) in total.

8. Your (chilled) puff pastry is now ready to use. Puff pastry will keep (wrapped) for up to 3 days in the fridge or 1 month in the freezer. As it is quite time-consuming, I always make a large block, then cut it down into smaller blocks to store in the freezer so I always have some ready to go. Defrost the pastry in the fridge before baking.

Quick Tip

To make a 'rough puff' pastry, replace steps 6 and 7 with a 'double turn' as follows: Roll the dough out vertically as before, but this time make it double the length. Then fold the top quarter down to the centre of the dough and the bottom quarter up to meet it. Then fold these two pieces together to close it like you would a book. Turn it 90 degrees, cover and rest in the fridge for 2 hours. Repeat the double turn and then cover and rest in the fridge for another 2 hours.

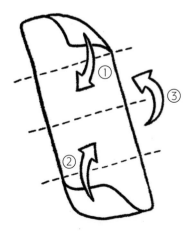

Bakes for

friends

One of the best things about baking is that it allows you to share your creations with others. People are always thrilled to receive something homemade – there's just so much love and care that goes into making something with your own two hands and giving it to someone else. It's a wonderful feeling.

However, when it comes to packaging up your treats, I find myself constantly buying Tupperware to transport baked goods all over town. I've learned to let go of the emotional attachment I used to have to my Tupperware containers and the guilt I would feel for not returning someone else's. It's all just part of the cycle of distribution.

These bakes are designed with friends in mind and are intended to give you some ideas for the next time you need to bring something to the office, a gathering, a picnic, or a friend in need. So go ahead and bake your heart out – your loved ones will thank you for it!

COFFEE, CARDAMOM AND WALNUT TRAYBAKE

SERVES 12

Equipment
28 x 18 x 5cm (11 x 7 x 2in) baking tin

For the cake
20g instant coffee

10g/2 tsp Camp Chicory and Coffee Essence (optional)

150ml hot water

5 green cardamom pods

125g soft light brown sugar

100g caster sugar

300g plain flour

1½ tsp baking powder

1 tsp bicarbonate of soda

pinch of fine salt

2 eggs

150ml buttermilk

150ml neutral oil, such as sunflower, vegetable or rapeseed oil, plus extra for greasing

For the topping
150g unsalted butter, at room temperature

50g icing sugar, sifted

250g cream cheese, at room temperature

20ml maple syrup, plus extra for drizzling

50g roasted walnut halves (see *Quick Tip*), roughly broken up into pieces

pinch of Maldon or flaky salt

Quick Tip

To roast the walnut halves, preheat the oven to 150°C fan/170°C/gas mark 3½. Put the walnuts on a rimmed baking tray in a single layer and roast for 13–15 minutes until golden brown, keeping an eye on them. Remove from the oven and cool, then roughly break up into pieces.

This coffee and cardamom cake base is loosely based on a cake I'm a bit in love with. It's from Honey & Co in London and it's just what you want from a coffee cake. It's delicate and full of flavour. This is a traybake version that stays soft for days.

Preheat the oven to 160°C fan/180°C/gas mark 4. Lightly grease and line the bottom and sides of the baking tin with baking paper.

Make the cake. Add the instant coffee and chicory and coffee essence (if using) to the hot water and stir to combine. Set aside.

Crush the cardamom pods to release the seeds, then crush the seeds to a powder using a pestle and mortar.

In a large bowl, stir together both sugars, the flour, baking powder, bicarbonate of soda, salt and the crushed cardamom seeds.

In another bowl, whisk together the instant coffee mix, the eggs, buttermilk and oil.

Pour the wet ingredients into the dry ingredients and use a whisk to combine until a smooth batter forms. Pour the batter into the prepared tin and spread evenly.

Bake for 30–35 minutes or until a skewer inserted into the centre comes out clean.

Remove from the oven and leave to cool completely in the tin. Once cool, remove the cake from the tin and place on a serving platter/board.

For the topping, beat the butter in a bowl until it's pliable, then mix through the icing sugar. Quickly mix through the cream cheese and maple syrup until it's homogeneous.

Spread the top of the cake generously with the topping, then use the back of a spoon to create little craters to house the walnuts. Scatter the walnuts over, then finish with an extra drizzle of maple syrup and a sprinkling of flaky salt. Cut into 12 portions and serve.

This traybake keeps well in an airtight container in the fridge for up to 4 days.

HAZELNUT AND CHOCOLATE COOKIES

MAKES 6 LARGE COOKIES

Equipment
large flat baking tray

235g plain flour

100g golden caster sugar

50g soft light brown sugar

25g cornflour

½ tsp baking powder

½ tsp bicarbonate of soda

¼ tsp Maldon or flaky salt

150g unsalted butter, melted

1 egg

1 egg yolk

50g blanched whole hazelnuts, roasted (see page 84), cooled and chopped in half

100g dark chocolate (70 per cent cocoa solids), roughly chopped (or use dark chocolate chips)

100g milk chocolate (40–55 per cent cocoa solids), roughly chopped (or use milk chocolate chips)

When you've got a long journey ahead of you, make these. You'll thank yourself when you reach into your bag and find one. I do this and it transports me to a feeling of immediate joy, satisfaction, pleasure and comfort.

In a large bowl, or the bowl of a stand mixer fitted with the paddle attachment, mix together the flour, both sugars, the cornflour, baking powder, bicarbonate of soda and salt. Add in the melted butter, egg and egg yolk and mix until a dough forms. Mix through the hazelnuts and both lots of chopped chocolate (or chocolate chips) until they are evenly distributed throughout the dough.

Portion into six large balls (each about 150g) and place on a tray. Refrigerate for 4 hours or freeze for 2 hours.

Preheat the oven to 170°C fan/190°C/gas mark 5. Line the baking tray with baking paper.

Transfer the chilled balls to the lined baking tray, pressing each one down slightly and leaving ample space between each one (as they will spread during baking).

Bake for 15 minutes or until they have spread and are golden on the edges.

Remove from the oven and allow the cookies to cool completely on the baking tray before eating.

Store the cookies in an airtight container at room temperature for up to 3 days.

DOUBLE CREAM FRANGIPANE/CHERRY BAKEWELL

Equipment

20cm (8in) round tart tin, 2.5cm (1in) deep; sturdy flat baking tray

For the pastry

90g plain flour, plus extra for dusting

1 tsp cornflour

pinch of fine salt

30g caster sugar

45g cold unsalted butter, cubed, plus extra (softened) for greasing

1 egg yolk

1–2 tbsp water

For the frangipane

135ml double cream

1 egg

2g/scant ½ tsp Maldon or flaky salt

100g golden caster sugar

30g soft light brown sugar

120g ground almonds

50g plain flour

For the cherry layer

50g cherry jam

15–20 fresh cherries or Griotte cherries from a jar (drained), pitted

20g flaked almonds

30g apricot jam

1 tbsp water

There is a running theme in my life and that's double cream. My friends laugh at me when I'm in the shop because I'll always pick up an entire tray of double cream and walk to the till with it – it's become a running joke for them. For me, I just always need cream, either for serving with puddings or for using in recipes – there's always someone on their way over you see and it's a shame not to be able to pour double cream over a pudding for them.

This frangipane is considerably lighter than its butter counterpart. It allows the almonds to shine and the flavour is really good. I made this one night because, to no surprise to anyone, I only had double cream in the fridge.

Make the pastry. In a large bowl or the bowl of a stand mixer or food processor, mix together the flour, cornflour, salt and sugar. Add the cold cubed butter and mix to breadcrumbs either with your fingertips, the paddle attachment or pulsed in the food processor. Add in the egg yolk and 1 tablespoon of the water. Mix briefly to form a loose dough – if it's really dry, add the second tablespoon of water and bring it together. Tip it out onto your work surface and knead gently to bring it together fully. Wrap tightly in clingfilm or baking paper and press to flatten into a disc. Refrigerate for 2 hours or until firm.

Grease the tart tin with a little soft unsalted butter. Lightly dust your workbench with flour. Remove the pastry from the fridge and gently knead it so the temperature of the middle is the same as the outside (this prevents it from breaking as you roll). Often this is where people go wrong, pressing down firmly onto COLD dough will cause it to tear and split. Roll it out to a round with a thickness of 4–5mm (¼in). Gently place this into the greased tart tin. Using your thumbs and the back of your fingers, press the pastry up the sides of the tin – there will be some overhang. Make sure the pastry is sitting snug in the tin and that there are no gaps along the sides. Refrigerate for 20 minutes.

Preheat the oven to 165°C fan/185°C/gas mark 4½. Place the sturdy flat baking tray on a rack/shelf in the middle of the oven to preheat (this helps to brown the bottom of the tart).

Blind-bake the pastry shell. Line the pastry shell with a sheet of baking paper, then fill to the top with baking beans or dried rice/lentils (it's important you fill to the top). Place it on the baking tray in the oven and bake for 20 minutes. Carefully remove the paper and baking beans, then return to the oven (on the baking tray) for a further 5–7 minutes or until it's nice and golden all over. Remove from the oven.

Continued overleaf →

DOUBLE CREAM FRANGIPANE/ CHERRY BAKEWELL *continued*

Meanwhile, make the frangipane. In a bowl, lightly whisk the cream, egg and salt together. Stir in both sugars. Add in the ground almonds and flour and stir well to combine. It is now ready to use. If made in advance, this will keep in a covered bowl in the fridge for 3–4 days.

Spread a layer of cherry jam over the base of the tart case. Pipe the frangipane into the tart in one even layer or spoon it in and smooth over with the back of the spoon. Add the cherries on top – I like to dot them around, thinking about how I'm going to portion it and making sure everyone will get a piece with enough cherries. Sprinkle the flaked almonds on top.

Bake (on the baking tray) for 35 minutes (at the same temperature) or until the top is golden and it doesn't jiggle.

Remove from the oven and allow to cool in the tin.

To finish, warm up the apricot jam with the water (in a small pan or microwave) and brush this over the tart.

Serve the tart slightly warm. It's also excellent for the next 2 days served at room temperature (store in an airtight container).

'There is a running theme in my life and that's double cream.'

MILLIONAIRE'S SHORTBREAD WITH PISTACHIO AND CARDAMOM

MAKES 12 LARGE PIECES OR 24 SMALL PIECES

Equipment

28 x 18 x 5cm (11 x 7 x 2in) baking tin

For the shortbread

250g plain flour

100g golden caster sugar

1 tbsp cornflour

2g/scant ½ tsp Maldon or flaky salt

20g ground pistachios

170g cold unsalted butter, cubed, plus extra (softened) for greasing

15ml neutral oil, such as sunflower, vegetable or rapeseed oil

For the caramel

200g caster sugar

200g golden syrup

90g unsalted butter

300ml double cream

2.5g/ ½ tsp Maldon or flaky salt

2 green cardamom pods, cracked open, seeds removed and crushed

For the chocolate topping

200g dark chocolate (70 per cent cocoa solids)

100g milk chocolate (40–55 per cent cocoa solids)

15ml neutral oil

When creating this millionaire's shortbread, I knew what I wanted it to 'eat like'. Crunchy, crisp shortbread, dark, deep, thick caramel and snappy, salty dark chocolate. When working on this I knew I wanted to avoid a pale shortbread and I didn't want it to be overly sickly sweet or claggy. Through my trials I found that using condensed milk to make the caramel produced a very sweet caramel that was susceptible to catching, so it needed constant attention. I also found it counterintuitive to add extra brown sugar to an already sweet condensed milk. The type that hurts your teeth. Instead, I resorted back to achieving a depth of flavour through directly caramelizing sugar on the hob with the addition of golden syrup to help with the texture. The difference being that it doesn't catch and it doesn't need constant whisking.

The shortbread is finished with chocolate and oil – this way you won't need to temper the chocolate, which is something I really don't enjoy doing when I'm at home. Melting chocolate with oil helps it to have that snappy texture, with a lot less fuss!

Preheat the oven to 170°C fan/190°C/gas mark 5. Lightly grease and line the cake tin with baking paper over the bottom and up the sides – the paper will be used to lift the shortbread out of the tin once it's ready, so it's important to use a long piece lengthways and another piece widthways.

Make the shortbread. In a large bowl, the bowl of a stand mixer fitted with the paddle attachment, or in a food processor, mix/pulse together the flour, sugar, cornflour, salt and ground pistachios. Add the cold cubed butter and rub in/mix/pulse to create breadcrumbs. Add the oil and briefly mix.

Tip this into the prepared tin, then use a small step palette knife to press it down in an even layer. Dock the shortbread all over using a fork (this helps to release steam during baking).

Continued overleaf →

Bake for 20 minutes or until golden. I really like a golden brown shortbread for a millionaire's shortbread rather than a pale blonde one, as I think it helps to balance the caramel and chocolate without it becoming sickly.

Remove from the oven and use the small step palette knife to press the shortbread down to compact it while it's warm, then leave to cool completely in the tin.

Make the caramel (see *Quick Tip*). In a large saucepan, heat the sugar and golden syrup together over a medium heat until the mixture is dark, deep and rich in colour and really fluid (this should take 6–9 minutes over a medium-high heat – keep a constant eye on it as it can start to burn very quickly). You can stir this occasionally. Whisk in the butter until it's incorporated, then slowly whisk in the cream (be careful as it might spit – wear long sleeves, as hot caramel can burn your skin). Stir in the salt and crushed cardamom seeds. Continue cooking the mixture over a medium-low heat, whisking occasionally, until it is reduced by about a third or it registers 121°C/249°F on a sugar thermometer. Pour the caramel directly over the shortbread in an even layer. Allow to cool completely at room temperature, about 2–3 hours.

For the chocolate topping, break both chocolates into pieces, then place in a heatproof bowl and melt together, either over a bain-marie (place the bowl over a pan of gently simmering water, making sure the bowl doesn't touch the water underneath) or in a microwave on medium power in 30-second bursts, stirring occasionally or after each burst. It needs to be just melted and it shouldn't be too hot. Add the oil and mix well to combine.

Pour this over the cooled caramel and leave to set at room temperature – this will take approx. 6–8 hours.

Once the chocolate layer has set, use the lining paper to lift it out of the tin onto a chopping board, then use a hot knife to cut the shortbread into portions.

These will keep in an airtight container at room temperature for up to 3 days.

Quick Tip

I highly recommend having all the ingredients weighed out and ready to go before you start making the caramel – timing is of the essence here and you'll want to make sure you have your full attention on what's going on in the pan so that the caramel does not burn.

CHERRY PIE

MAKES 1 X 20CM (8IN) PIE;
SERVES 6–8

This is a proper cherry pie and I make it every summer. It's a recipe I've come to really look forward to as the seasons change.

Equipment

20cm (8in) round pie tin/dish
or cake tin, 5cm (2in) deep;
baking tray; heavy baking tray

For the pastry

225g strong white flour, plus extra
   for dusting

5g/1 tsp fine salt

15g/1 tbsp caster sugar

175g cold unsalted butter, cubed, plus
   extra (softened) for greasing

70ml ice-cold water

For the cherry filling

about 520g fresh cherries (you'll need
   500g pitted cherries) (see *Quick Tips*)

180g golden caster sugar

¼ tsp almond extract/Disaronno or
   amaretto liqueur (optional)

50g cornflour

To finish

2 tbsp full-fat milk, for brushing

1 tbsp demerara sugar, for sprinkling

Make the pastry. In a large bowl or the bowl of a stand mixer fitted with the paddle attachment, mix the flour, salt and caster sugar together. Add in the cold cubed butter and rub in or mix until you have a breadcrumb texture (you still want to be able to see some small chunks of butter). Add in the ice-cold water in one go and mix quickly to form a dough.

Tip the dough out onto your work surface and bring together with your hands into a flat disc. Wrap tightly in clingfilm and refrigerate for at least 2 hours or until firm.

Meanwhile, make the cherry filling. Pit the cherries (keeping them whole) and place them in a large bowl (the weight of cherries post-pitting should be 500g). Toss the cherries in the caster sugar, almond extract/Disaronno (if using) and the cornflour. Set aside while you prepare the pie case. There may be some juice that leaches out from the cherries, but don't worry too much, that's what the cornflour will help with (see *Quick Tips*).

Grease the pie tin/dish or cake tin with a little butter. Gently knead the chilled pastry dough a bit, then cut a third off and keep it aside for the lid. On a lightly floured work surface, roll out the remaining pastry to 4mm (¼in) thickness and line the prepared tin/dish with the pastry, leaving a bit of an overhang. Keep the scraps if you have any and add these to the pastry for the lid. Put the pastry-lined tin/dish in the fridge.

Line the baking tray with baking paper. Roll out the reserved lid pastry to 4mm (¼in) thickness and either cut a lattice (see *Quick Tips*) or leave it whole, then transfer to the lined baking tray and chill in the fridge for 15 minutes.

Continued overleaf →

CHERRY PIE *continued*

Once the case and lid are cold, add the cherry mixture to the pie case and top with the lid. Pinch around the top edge of the pie to seal, trimming then fluting the edges as you pinch, if you like. If the lid is being left whole, pierce a hole in the top with a sharp knife. Return to the fridge for 10 minutes.

Preheat the oven to 200°C fan/220°C/gas mark 7. Put the heavy baking tray in the oven to heat up – it works best on the very bottom shelf/rack of the oven.

To finish, brush the top of the pie with the milk and sprinkle with the demerara sugar. Transfer the pie to the baking tray in the oven. Bake for 30 minutes, then reduce the oven temperature to 180°C fan/200°C/gas mark 6 and bake for a further 45 minutes, until golden brown.

Remove from the oven and allow the pie to cool slightly before serving with ice cream, custard or cream, or in Jeremy Lee-style, ALL THREE.

This pie is best served warm but it can also be enjoyed cold. It will keep in an airtight container in the fridge for up to 3 days (reheat in a hot oven, if desired).

Quick Tips

You can use frozen cherries for this recipe, however, it is essential that they are fully defrosted before using. Once they are fully defrosted, strain off the excess liquid and then toss in the sugar, almond extract/liqueur (if using) and cornflour.

The cherries will leach out a bit of juice once they've been tossed in the sugar and cornflour but this is a good thing, it makes the filling nice and juicy. The cornflour will also mingle and do its thing in the oven and turn that juice into a lovely sauce.

To prepare a lattice, cut eight strips approx. 5–7.5cm (2–3in) wide (each long enough to fit over the pie filling), using the scraps and re-rolling them to create all the strips, if needed. Put these on a tray and chill in the fridge for 15 minutes before using them to create a lattice on top of the pie. To do this, line up four strips vertically and four horizontally with a little space between each one, then weave each strip alternately over and under each other to create a lattice effect.

COFFEE CHOUX

MAKES 13–14 CHOUX BUNS

Equipment
2 flat baking trays

For the coffee crème mousseline
500ml full-fat milk

120g caster sugar

2 tbsp instant coffee

pinch of Maldon or flaky salt

40g cornflour

6 egg yolks

1 tsp vanilla bean paste (optional)

150g unsalted butter, at room
    temperature

For the craquelin
75g unsalted butter, softened

75g demerara sugar

75g strong white flour

pinch of Maldon or flaky salt

For the choux pastry
100ml water

100ml full-fat milk

100g unsalted butter

5g/1 tsp caster sugar

2g/scant ½ tsp fine salt

100g strong white flour

3–4 eggs

icing sugar, for dusting

When I decided to become a pastry chef, I would dream of living in Paris, working there and eating my way around all of the patisseries. Instead, I never quite had the guts to move to Paris with my limited French language, so instead I visited once a year for a while doing the eating bit without the living there bit. To this day, something that has always stood out for me was a coffee éclair I ate at a small patisserie, it wasn't an éclair as I knew it to be, but a filled light choux bun stuffed full with coffee cream. This is my take on those delicious coffee choux buns.

First, make the coffee crème mousseline. In a medium saucepan, heat the milk with half the sugar, the instant coffee and salt over a medium heat until steaming.

In a small bowl, mix together the cornflour and the remaining sugar. Whisk the egg yolks in a separate heatproof bowl with the vanilla (if using) before whisking in the cornflour/sugar mix until combined.

When the milk is steaming, pour it over the egg yolk mixture and whisk well. Return to the pan and whisk vigorously over a medium heat until thick and bubbling, about 4–5 minutes.

Remove from the heat and pour into a large heatproof bowl, add the butter, then use a stick blender to blitz it all together until combined. Tip into another clean heatproof bowl or container, then place a sheet of clingfilm directly on the surface (to prevent a skin forming). Leave to cool, then chill in the fridge for a minimum of 4 hours, until thickened.

Meanwhile, make the craquelin. In a medium bowl, mix together the butter, demerara sugar and flour until a dough is formed. Tip this out onto a sheet of baking paper, top with another sheet of baking paper, then roll out to 3–4mm (⅛–¼in) thickness. Put this on a tray and chill in the fridge for 1 hour or until set like a sheet of biscuit.

Use a 4cm (1½in) round biscuit cutter to cut out 13–14 discs of craquelin to fit directly onto the piped choux pastry (see overleaf) – they should be just a touch smaller, so 4cm (1½in) will work well. Any scraps can be re-rolled or wrapped in clingfilm and frozen for up to 1 month (defrost before use).

Meanwhile, make the choux. In a medium saucepan, combine the water, milk, butter, caster sugar and salt. Bring to a rolling boil (this is key), then turn the heat down slightly and add the flour in one go. Use a sturdy wooden spoon or heatproof spoon and mix this vigorously until the mixture comes away from the sides of the pan.

Continued overleaf →

COFFEE CHOUX *continued*

Stir for 3–4 minutes over a medium heat, then remove from the heat and tip into either the bowl of a stand mixer or a large heatproof bowl. Leave to cool for about 15 minutes, before you start adding the eggs. In a separate bowl, whisk together the eggs.

Using the paddle attachment or an electric handheld whisk, start adding the whisked eggs to the choux mixture in the bowl, mixing as you go. You are looking for the mixture to turn glossy, smooth and to be at 'dropping consistency' – meaning you should be able to lift the mixture out of the bowl on a spoon and with a very gentle nudge it should drop from the spoon. It shouldn't run off the spoon or cling to it. You may not need to add all the eggs, so add them gradually and check the consistency once you've added about 3 eggs.

Preheat the oven to 190°C fan/210°C/gas mark 6½. Line the baking trays with baking paper. Sometimes it's helpful to place a tiny magnet on each corner of the paper to hold it down as the choux is quite light. Alternatively, use silicone baking mats, as choux bakes really nicely on these.

Spoon the choux mixture into a piping bag fitted with a 1cm (½in) round nozzle. Pipe 5cm (2in) rounds onto the lined baking trays, leaving enough room between each for them to grow. Top each choux bun with a disc of the craquelin.

Bake for 17 minutes, then reduce the oven temperature to 170°C fan/190°C/gas mark 5 and bake for a further 15 minutes. The choux buns should easily lift off the paper when they are ready and they should feel light to touch, hollow and crisp.

Remove from the oven. Take a round piping nozzle and use the tip of the nozzle to create a hole in the base of each choux bun – this will be used as the point of entry to pipe the mousseline in later and doing this now helps to release excess steam. Transfer to a wire rack and cool completely.

When you are ready to serve, briefly whip the mousseline to give it a lighter texture and make it easy to pipe. Spoon the mousseline into a piping bag fitting with a 1cm (½in) round nozzle. Fill each choux bun with the mousseline by inserting the nozzle into the bottom of each one and pressing on the bag. Once each choux bun is filled, place it bottom-side down onto a serving plate.

Dust the choux buns with icing sugar and serve immediately.

Once filled, these choux buns will keep in an airtight container in the fridge for up to 2 days but they will soften.

MANDARIN, ALMOND AND POLENTA CAKE

MAKES 1 X 20CM (8IN) CAKE; SERVES 8-10

Equipment
20cm (8in) deep round cake tin

For the cake
180g fresh mandarin oranges
unsalted butter, for greasing
200g caster sugar
3 eggs
120ml neutral oil, such as sunflower, vegetable or rapeseed oil
100g ground almonds
100g fine polenta
2½ tsp baking powder
pinch of Maldon or flaky salt
juice of ½ lemon

For the sugar syrup
25g caster sugar
2 tbsp water
juice of 1 lemon

This cake works really well with mandarins because their skin is quite thin. If you use an orange with a thicker amount of pith, the resulting cake will be rather bitter. It stays wonderfully soft, fragrant and moist and can also be baked as smaller individual cakes in a greased 12-hole muffin tin – simply adjust the baking time to 18–20 minutes.

Make the cake. Wipe the mandarin oranges with a clean wet cloth to remove any dirt. Place the mandarins in a large deep saucepan, add enough water to cover them, then use a small plate or a smaller lid placed directly on top to keep them pressed down under the liquid.

Bring to a gentle simmer over a medium heat and cook for about 30–40 minutes or until when the mandarins are pierced with a sharp knife, it meets little resistance. Remove from the heat and drain off the water. Set aside.

Preheat the oven to 160°C fan/180°C/gas mark 4. Lightly grease the cake tin with butter and line it with baking paper.

Blend the mandarins in their skins in a high-speed blender until a smooth pulp forms, then scrape this into a bowl.

In another bowl, whisk the sugar and eggs together until combined. Add the oil and whisk well. In a separate bowl, stir together the ground almonds, polenta, baking powder and salt.

Add the dry ingredients to the whisked egg mixture and stir well to combine. Finally, stir through the blitzed mandarin pulp and follow this with the lemon juice. Scrape the mixture into the prepared tin, spreading it level.

Bake for 45–50 minutes or until a skewer inserted into the centre comes out clean.

Remove from the oven and allow the cake to cool completely in the tin.

Make the syrup. In a small saucepan, heat the sugar, water and lemon juice together over a medium heat until the sugar has dissolved, bring this to the boil, then remove from the heat. Use it warm.

Pierce the top of the cold cake all over with a skewer, then carefully pour over the warm syrup (do the same if you have made smaller individual cakes in a muffin tin – see intro). Let this sit for 10 minutes, then remove the cake from the tin and serve in slices with a dollop of whipped cream.

This cake will keep in an airtight container at room temperature for up to 3 days.

BROWNIES

**MAKES 15 SMALL
BROWNIES**

Equipment

24 x 16 x 3cm (9½ x 6¼ x 1¼ in) baking tin

120g unsalted butter, plus extra for
    greasing
200g dark chocolate (70 per cent cocoa
    solids), roughly chopped
2 eggs
2g/scant ½ tsp Maldon or flaky salt
100g caster sugar
100g soft dark brown sugar
40g plain flour
40g dark chocolate chips, chunks, or a bar
    of chocolate of your choice chopped
    into 1cm (½in) pieces
15 pitted fresh or canned (drained)
    cherries

As a pastry chef, I would describe a big part of my diet as 'brownie trimmings'. Every morning shift I'd try to say to myself this is the day where I don't, I don't eat brownie off-cuts for breakfast. Yet I'd find myself at that mid-morning dip stage, stomach rumbling with a while to go before my break, looking lovingly at those brownie trimmings and I'd go, ok just for today then.

Allan Jenkins declared them 'the best brownies he'd had in a long time' by way of Holly O'Neill at the OFM offices after giving her some of my recipe tests to try.

Preheat the oven to 165°C fan/185°C/gas mark 4½. Lightly grease and line the baking tin with baking paper.

Melt the butter in a heatproof bowl, either in short bursts in a microwave or over a bain-marie until fully melted (this will help the chocolate to melt quickly).

Add the 200g of roughly chopped chocolate and stir until homogeneous, adding a little heat if needed, either by placing the bowl back over the bain-marie for a little bit or by applying short bursts of heat in the microwave. Stir well.

In a separate large bowl, whisk the eggs, salt and both sugars together until fully combined. Pour in the melted butter and chocolate mixture, mix well to combine.

Using a whisk, stir in the flour until there are no bits of flour visible, then switch to a large spoon and stir in the chocolate chips/chunks/pieces. Scoop this mixture into the prepared tin, spreading it level, then evenly distribute the cherries on top.

Bake for 20 minutes or until the edges look like they are starting to dry slightly but the middle is still fudgy.

Remove from the oven and allow to cool completely in the tin before placing in the fridge to chill completely – this is key. Slice into 15 portions and serve.

These brownies keep in an airtight container in the fridge for 3–4 days – enjoy slightly cold! They can also be frozen once baked, if tightly wrapped, for up to 1 month. Defrost at room temperature. These work very well as gifts.

FIG, RICOTTA AND HONEY CAKE

MAKES 1 X 20CM (8IN)
CAKE; SERVES 8–10

This cake is inspired by the most sublime fig, ricotta and honey gelato I have ever eaten in Bologna, which I watched being spooned out of the machine into a cup for me as I waited patiently for it, having had a breakfast gelato and come back eagerly for more after lunch. I am that person. Make this when the figs are good and the sun is shining.

Equipment

20cm (8in) deep round cake tin

For the figs

8 ripe figs (about 300g total weight), quartered

40g soft light brown sugar

splash of water

For the cake

150g unsalted butter, softened, plus extra for greasing

180g caster sugar

40g light honey (runny ideally), plus extra for drizzling

pinch of fine salt

3 eggs

1½ tsp baking powder

150g plain flour

40g ground almonds

250g ricotta

icing sugar, for dusting

First, prepare the figs by heating them with the brown sugar and water in a pan over a low-medium heat, stirring occasionally, until the figs break down, about 15 minutes. Remove the pan from the heat and allow the figs to cool before using.

Preheat the oven to 165°C fan/185°C/gas mark 4½. Lightly grease and line the bottom and sides of the cake tin with baking paper.

For the cake, in a large bowl or the bowl of a stand mixer fitted with the paddle attachment, beat the butter, caster sugar, honey and salt together until light and fluffy. Add the eggs, one by one, and mix well. Add the baking powder and mix thoroughly. Mix in the flour and ground almonds until homogeneous. Add the cooled figs and mix well to combine. Finally, gently stir through the ricotta until combined. Pour into the prepared cake tin and level the top.

Bake for 45–60 minutes or until a skewer inserted into the centre comes out clean.

Remove from the oven and allow to cool completely in the tin before turning out.

Place the cake on a serving plate. Drizzle the top of the cake with honey and dust with icing sugar to serve and dollop over a little crème fraîche or whipped double cream.

This cake will keep in an airtight container at room temperature for up to 3 days.

PECAN PIE

I didn't know I liked pecan pie until I tried chef PJ's version at Vadas Bakery in Cape Town – it was unlike any version of a pecan pie that I'd tried before. Not too sweet, silky, light and, most importantly, stuffed full of roasted pecans.

It took me several attempts to bake a version that I was happy with. It went from a bourbon caramel (like PJ's) to a set caramel, with different pastry styles each time. In the end, I settled on a really simple salted-cream filling – a light brown sugar mix with a lot of pecans. It's vastly different to PJ's but I think it's capable of converting any pecan pie naysayer.

Equipment

20cm (8in) round tart tin, fluted or straight-edged; sturdy flat baking tray

For the pastry

125g plain flour, plus extra for dusting

pinch of Maldon or flaky salt

1 tbsp caster sugar

80g cold unsalted butter, cubed, plus extra (softened) for greasing

30ml ice cold water

1 egg, beaten, for sealing pastry case (optional)

cold water

For the filling

75g soft light brown sugar

75g caster sugar

large pinch of Maldon or flaky salt

2 eggs

300ml double cream

50g unsalted butter, melted

200g pecans, roasted (see *Quick Tip* for roasting walnuts on page 27) and roughly chopped

Make the pastry. In a large bowl, or the bowl of a stand mixer fitted with the paddle attachment, mix the flour, salt and caster sugar together. Add in the cold cubed butter and rub in or mix until you have a breadcrumb texture (you still want to be able to see some small chunks of butter). Add in the ice-cold water in one go and mix quickly to form a dough. Tip onto your workbench and knead briefly before wrapping in clingfilm and chilling in the fridge for 2 hours or until firm.

Lightly grease the bottom of the tart tin with butter and line with a circle of baking paper.

On a lightly floured surface, roll out the pastry to a round, 3–4mm (⅛–¼in) thickness. Use the pastry to line the prepared tart tin, making sure you push the pastry into the inner edges and leave an overhang. Refrigerate for 30 minutes.

Preheat the oven to 160°C fan/180°C/gas mark 4. Place the sturdy baking tray on a shelf/rack in the centre of the oven to preheat.

Blind-bake the pastry. Line the pastry case with a sheet of baking paper and fill to the top with baking beans or dried rice/lentils. Put this on the preheated baking tray in the oven and bake for 20–25 minutes or until the edges are lightly golden. Carefully remove the baking paper and beans, then return to the oven (on the baking tray) for 18–20 minutes until the base is golden.

Meanwhile, make the filling. In a large bowl, mix the soft brown sugar, caster sugar, salt, eggs and cream together, add the melted butter and fold in the chopped pecans.

Continued overleaf →

PECAN PIE *continued*

Remove the blind-baked pastry case from the oven and if there are any holes or cracks, brush with a little extra beaten egg before returning to the oven again briefly for 2–3 minutes to seal it.

Turn the oven down to 150°C fan/170°C/gas mark 3½.

Pour the pecan filling evenly into the pastry case, then bake (on the baking tray) for 25–30 minutes until the top is golden all over, but there is still a slight wobble in the middle.

Remove from the oven and allow to cool in the tin. While it is still slightly warm, use a small serrated knife to tidy up the edges of the pie and cut off any excess pastry. Leave the pie to cool completely in the tin.

Remove from the tart tin and serve the pecan pie in slices with whipped cream, crème fraîche or ice cream.

The pecan pie will keep in an airtight container at room temperature for up to 3 days.

'It's capable of converting any pecan pie naysayer.'

PISTACHIO FINANCIERS

MAKES 12

Equipment
12-cup silicone financier mould/tin
or similar (see intro)

60g ground almonds

40g ground pistachios, plus 20g flaked
   pistachios, extra for topping (optional)

20g plain flour

pinch of fine salt

¼ tsp baking powder

90g icing sugar, plus extra for dusting

3 egg whites (approx. 85g)

75g unsalted butter, melted and cooled,
   plus extra (softened or melted) for
   greasing

I'm a sucker for a delicate financier, especially with a coffee. These are really easy to make, they are a great way of using up egg whites and they keep really well in an airtight container for up to 5 days.

These can be baked in small silicone moulds or mini loaf tin moulds, or you can bake them in any sort of individual shaped tins that you have. The key is to just make sure you grease them and fill with batter to just above halfway, then bake until a skewer inserted into the centre comes out clean.

Preheat the oven to 180°C fan/200°C/gas mark 6. Grease the financier mould/tin with butter and place in the fridge while you make the batter.

In a medium bowl, mix together the dry ingredients (ground almonds and pistachios, flour, salt, baking powder and icing sugar) with a whisk to fully combine. Sift this into another bowl using a medium sieve.

Pour the egg whites and melted butter over the dry ingredients, then use the whisk to combine everything until it turns into a batter.

Divide the mixture evenly between the greased cups, filling each one just above halfway.

Bake for 15–18 minutes or until golden and a skewer inserted into the centre of each cake comes out clean.

Remove from the oven and leave to cool in the mould/tin for 5 minutes, then remove and transfer to a wire rack to cool completely.

Sprinkle over a few flaked pistashios, if you like, and dust the financiers with icing sugar just before serving. Serve with mugs of steaming coffee and enjoy.

These will keep in an airtight container at room temperature for up to 5 days.

DUTCH SHORTCAKES

MAKES 10

Equipment
flat baking tray

150g unsalted butter, softened

1 tsp vanilla bean paste

pinch of Maldon or flaky salt

175g plain flour

25g cornflour

40g icing sugar

2 tbsp full-fat milk

100g dark chocolate (70 per cent cocoa solids) or milk chocolate (40–55 per cent cocoa solids), melted (optional)

Unlike traditional biscuit dough, these biscuits are made using a soft dough that's piped into swirls or batons before being baked. The key to getting a nice shape is to make sure the dough is soft enough to pipe, and that's where the addition of milk helps.

If it's a particularly cold day, you can definitely warm the biscuit mixture very gently either in short bursts in the microwave (on medium power) or really carefully over a bain-marie. The goal isn't to melt the butter but more to soften the mixture so it doesn't break the piping bag or break as you pipe it. Once you've piped the biscuits, put them in the fridge to set again, as this lowers the risk of them spreading as they bake.

Dipping the baked biscuits into melted chocolate is optional, by the way, you can just eat them as they are, if you prefer. If you like sweeter biscuits, then use milk chocolate!

Preheat the oven to 160°C fan/180°C/gas mark 4. Line the baking tray with baking paper.

In a large bowl or the bowl of a stand mixer fitted with the paddle attachment, beat the butter with the vanilla and salt until completely smooth.

In a separate bowl, stir together the flour, cornflour and icing sugar. Add the dry ingredients to the creamed butter and mix really well. Finally, add in the milk and mix well. The mixture should be pipeable, so if it's too firm (see intro), you can really gently warm the mixture in short bursts in the microwave on medium power (or very carefully over a bain-marie) – but only slightly!

Fit a star-shaped nozzle (I used 1M) into a piping bag and spoon in the biscuit mixture. Pipe 10 swirls or batons of the mixture onto the lined baking tray, leaving a little space between each one. (If it's a cold day and you had to gently warm the mixture before piping, put the piped biscuits in the fridge to set again before baking – see intro.)

Bake for 10–12 minutes until lightly golden.

Remove from the oven and allow to cool completely on the baking tray before eating.

If you'd like to dip the biscuits in chocolate, line a tray with baking paper. Dip half of each biscuit in the melted chocolate, transfer to the lined tray, then place in the fridge to set before serving.

These biscuits keep well in an airtight container at room temperature for up to 3 days.

PANTRY RAID FLAPJACKS

MAKES 9

Equipment

24 x 16 x 3cm (9½ x 6¼ x 1¼in) baking tin

150g unsalted butter, plus extra for greasing

120g golden syrup

50ml apple juice

large pinch of Maldon or flaky salt

50g almond butter

200g jumbo oats

40g pumpkin seeds

40g dried blueberries

60g dried apricots, chopped into quarters

This is a good recipe for using up those odds and ends we often seem to accumulate, including various seeds, nuts and dried fruits. As long as they have been stored correctly, whatever you have to hand will be fine to use in place of the same quantities as below for fruit and/or nuts.

Preheat the oven to 160°C fan/180°C/gas mark 4. Lightly grease and line the baking tin with baking paper so that it comes up the sides, too.

In a medium saucepan, melt the butter, then stir in the golden syrup, apple juice, salt and almond butter.

In a heatproof bowl, stir together the oats, pumpkin seeds, blueberries and apricots.

Pour the warm butter mixture into the oat mixture and stir well with a wooden spoon to combine. Press the mixture into the lined baking tin in an even layer.

Bake for 25–30 minutes until it looks dry to touch and slightly golden.

Remove from the oven and cool slightly in the tin before cutting into nine portions, then leave to cool completely in the tin. Once cool, break into portions and serve.

Store leftovers in an airtight container at room temperature for up to 1 week.

FIG ROLLS

I am a snacker and am so at any opportunity, be that flight, road trip, wedding, whatever. I'll always make time to go to the shops and buy copious amounts of snacks to share. When I was at Uni, I got persuaded to go to a camping festival, so I left my friend in charge of the compulsory snack pilgrimage, only to find out all he bought were packets of fig rolls. Bizarre. He then got really high and shoved two whole packets of fig rolls into his mouth one after the other quickly. We were in stitches. I think he woke up the next day and realized his error. Whenever I make or eat fig rolls, I think of him.

'I am a snacker and am so at any opportunity.'

MAKES ABOUT 20

Equipment
large flat baking tray

For the dough
50g unsalted butter, at room temperature
50g caster sugar
1 egg
1 capful (approx. 5ml/1 tsp) of almond extract (optional)
150g plain flour, plus extra for dusting
30g ground almonds
¼ tsp baking powder
pinch of Maldon or flaky salt

For the fig filling
300ml water
30g soft light brown sugar
200g dried figs, stems removed and chopped
1 cinnamon stick

demerara sugar, for sprinkling

Make the dough. In a large bowl, beat the butter and caster sugar together until pale and fluffy. Mix in the egg, scraping down the sides of the bowl, along with the almond extract, if using.

In a separate bowl, mix the flour, ground almonds, baking powder and salt together. Add this to the butter mixture and mix until a dough forms. Knead for a minute or two until it's homogeneous.

Pat the dough into a disc, wrap in clingfilm or baking paper and refrigerate for 2 hours.

Meanwhile, make the fig filling. In a medium saucepan, stir together the water, brown sugar, figs and cinnamon stick. Bring this to a gentle simmer over a medium heat, stirring occasionally, then simmer until the water has reduced by half, about 10 minutes.

Remove the pan from the heat. Tip the fig mixture into a heatproof bowl and leave until it is cool to touch, then refrigerate until cold, approx. 20 minutes. Remove the cinnamon stick before using. Blitz to form a paste using a food processor.

Line a kitchen tray and the baking tray with baking paper and set aside.

On a lightly floured surface, roll out the dough to a rectangle 38 x 18cm (15 x 7in). Cut the strip in half lengthways. Place one strip on a large sheet of baking paper – this is going to help you roll it into shape.

Spoon the fig filling into a piping bag fitted with a large plain nozzle, then pipe half of the fig filling along the length, leaving about a 2cm (¾in) border on one side which will help you to close it. Use a pastry brush to brush water along this border. Use the baking paper to help lift the other side of the pastry over the filling and onto the dampened edge, as you would do when making sausage rolls. Use a fork to press down and seal the edges together. Place this on the lined kitchen tray and transfer to the fridge, then repeat with the second strip of pastry and the rest of the fig filling. Refrigerate for 20 minutes while the oven preheats.

Preheat the oven to 160°C fan/180°C/gas mark 4.

Use a sharp knife to cut across each long roll and portion the fig rolls – cutting each one to about 3–4cm (1¼–1½in) in size works nicely. Transfer the fig rolls to the lined baking tray, then brush them with a little water before sprinkling over a little demerara sugar.

Bake for 15–18 minutes or until golden.

Remove from the oven, cool slightly, then transfer to a wire rack to cool completely before serving.

Leftovers will keep in an airtight container at room temperature for up to 3 days.

CARROT CAKE

**MAKES 1 X 20CM (8IN)
CAKE; SERVES 8**

Equipment
2 x 20cm (8in) sandwich cake tins

For the cake
unsalted butter, for greasing

4 eggs

130g soft dark brown sugar

70g caster sugar

150ml neutral oil, such as sunflower,
vegetable or rapeseed oil

180g plain flour

1½ tsp baking powder

½ tsp bicarbonate of soda

½ tsp ground cinnamon

½ tsp smoked sea salt

350g carrots, grated (approx. 4 medium
carrots)

65g cored and grated cooking apple
(no need to peel)

1 tbsp Greek yogurt

50g pecans, roasted (see *Quick Tip* for
roasting walnuts on page 27) and
roughly chopped

45g rum-soaked raisins (see *Quick Tip*
on page 187), or raisins that have
been soaked in just-boiled water for
20 minutes and strained

For the frosting
200g unsalted butter, at room
temperature

100g maple syrup

400g cream cheese, at room temperature

large pinch of Maldon or flaky salt

20g pecans, roasted and chopped,
to decorate

The opposite of a dry cake, this carrot cake utilizes apple, yogurt and a little smoked sea salt. This works well either as a teatime cake or as a birthday cake. If you'd like to cover the sides of the cake as well as the top, I'd advise making another half quantity of the frosting to do this.

Preheat the oven to 160°C fan/180°C/gas mark 4. Lightly grease and line the two cake tins with baking paper.

Make the cake. In a large bowl, whisk the eggs and both sugars together until combined, then pour in the oil and mix well.

In a separate bowl, stir together the flour, baking powder, bicarbonate of soda, cinnamon and smoked sea salt.

Mix the dry ingredients through the egg mixture, then stir through the carrots and apple, followed by the yogurt, chopped pecans and rum/water-soaked raisins. Divide the mixture evenly between the two prepared tins and level the tops.

Bake for 35 minutes or until a skewer inserted into the centre of each cake comes out clean.

Remove from the oven and cool the cakes slightly in the tins, then turn out onto a wire rack to cool completely.

Make the frosting. In a large bowl, beat the butter with a wooden spoon (make sure the butter is completely soft – if it's hard at all there will be lumps in the frosting and you won't be able to rectify this later), then mix in the maple syrup. Fold in the cream cheese briefly but vigorously, then add the salt to finish and stir through. Use the frosting immediately.

Sandwich the cake together with half of the frosting, then spread the rest on the top of the cake, lifting it into decorative peaks, if you like. Decorate with the chopped pecans. Serve in slices.

This cake will keep in an airtight container in the fridge for up to 4 days.

FRUIT SCONES

MAKES 6 SCONES

Equipment
flat baking tray

15g/1 tbsp raisins
just-boiled water, to cover
250g plain flour, plus extra for dusting
12g/2½ tsp baking powder
¼ tsp fine salt
30g caster sugar
75g cold unsalted butter, cubed
25g (prepped weight) eating apple
    (approx. ¼ small apple), cored
    and grated
125ml full-fat milk
1 egg, beaten, for the egg wash

One of my earliest pastry jobs involved making hundreds of scones each morning for afternoon tea service. The key was never to overmix the dough and to get your hands involved to bring it together, then to rest it before cutting.

A scone is best served on the day it is baked with copious amounts of clotted cream and jam on the side.

Put the raisins in a small, heatproof bowl, cover with just-boiled water and leave to soak for 20 minutes, then drain.

In a large bowl, stir together the flour, baking powder, salt and sugar. Add the butter and use your fingertips to breadcrumb it together. Mix through the apple and strained raisins.

Keeping one hand out of the bowl, make a well in the centre and add the milk. Use your hand (that's in the bowl) to bring it together initially to a loose dough, but do not overwork it. Tip this onto your workbench and then use both hands to gently bring it together to form a dough. Gently shape into a disc, then wrap tightly in baking paper or clingfilm and refrigerate for 30 minutes.

Preheat the oven to 180°C fan/200°C/gas mark 6. Line the baking tray with baking paper.

Lightly dust your workbench and a 6.5cm (2¾in) round biscuit cutter with flour. Unwrap the chilled dough and gently roll it into a round, about 3cm (1¼in) thick. Position the cutter, then press down in one straight motion (don't twist the cutter) with your hand to cut out each scone, then gather the trimmings and cut out another scone.

Place the rounds on the lined baking tray, then brush the top of each one with egg wash.

Bake for 18–20 minutes or until risen and lightly golden.

Remove from the oven, transfer the scones to a wire rack and allow to cool fully before serving. Serve split and spread with butter and jam, or clotted cream and jam, or all three!

These scones are best eaten fresh on the day they are made.

MALTED CHOCOLATE AND PEANUT LOAF

MAKES 1 SMALL LOAF; SERVES 6–8

Equipment
1 x 1lb loaf tin

For the loaf cake
150g caster sugar

120g plain flour

1 tsp baking powder

½ tsp bicarbonate of soda

pinch of fine salt

20g cocoa powder

2 tbsp malt powder

2 eggs

70ml neutral oil, such as sunflower, vegetable or rapeseed oil, plus extra for greasing

90g Greek yoghurt or sour cream

50g peanut butter, preferably chunky and dark roast (optional)

For the topping
200g white chocolate (20 per cent cocoa butter), broken into small pieces or roughly chopped

100ml double cream

30g roasted, salted peanuts, roughly chopped

Gosh, this is a good loaf, fantastically easy to make and impressive at the same time. It looks like it's come straight out of a fancy bakery and has all of the textures one wants for a teatime loaf. The peanut butter filling is, of course, optional, but if you do choose to do this (and I encourage you to!), use a really nice quality chunky dark roast peanut butter so it's not cloying. Alternatively, use a filling of your choice such as chocolate spread.

Preheat the oven to 160°C fan/180°C/gas mark 4. Lightly grease and line the loaf tin with baking paper.

Make the loaf cake. In a large bowl, mix together the sugar, flour, baking powder, bicarbonate of soda, salt, cocoa powder and malt powder.

In a separate bowl, whisk together the eggs, oil and Greek yoghurt or sour cream. Pour this mixture into the dry ingredients and stir with a whisk until a smooth batter forms. Pour the batter into the prepared loaf tin and level the top. It should reach three-quarters of the way up the tin – do not overfill.

Bake for 40–45 minutes or until a skewer inserted into the centre comes out clean.

Remove from the oven and allow the loaf cake to cool completely in the tin, then turn out of the tin and peel off the lining paper.

Use an apple corer to create space in the centre of the loaf cake for the peanut butter filling (if using). I do this by inserting the corer horizontally all the way through the middle of the loaf, roughly 5cm (2in) up from the bottom (you can nibble on the pieces of cake removed from the centre!). Spoon the peanut butter into a piping bag fitted with a medium plain nozzle (or use a disposable piping bag and cut off the tip) and pipe it into the loaf through the hole you have just made to create a nice centre.

For the topping, gently melt the white chocolate with the double cream in a small pan over a low heat until combined, stirring occasionally. Stir in the chopped roasted peanuts.

Place the filled loaf on a wire rack and carefully pour the white chocolate mixture over the loaf so it covers the top completely and drips down the sides. Leave to set, then slice and serve.

This loaf keeps well in an airtight container at room temperature for up to 3 days.

BLUEBERRY MUFFIN CAKE

MAKES 1 X 15CM (6IN) CAKE; SERVES 6

This is a really simple and easy cake to put together, and is perfect for a relaxed afternoon shared with friends drinking mugs of tea. The batter is a little like muffin batter, but here it's baked as one cake to enjoy with friends.

Equipment
15cm (6in) sandwich cake tin

100g Greek yogurt
50g unsalted butter, melted and cooled, plus extra for greasing
1 egg
120g plain flour
5g/1 tsp baking powder
100g caster sugar
pinch of fine salt
finely grated zest of ½ lemon
100g fresh or frozen blueberries
40g white chocolate (20 per cent cocoa butter), chopped into small chunks

Preheat the oven to 160°C fan/180°C/gas mark 4. Lightly grease and line the cake tin with baking paper.

In a large bowl, whisk together the yogurt, melted butter and egg. In a separate bowl, stir together the flour, baking powder, sugar, salt and lemon zest.

Pour the egg mixture into the dry mixture and use a whisk to stir them together well until there are no lumps and the flour is fully incorporated. Finally, stir through the blueberries and white chocolate. Scoop this into the prepared cake tin and spread it level.

Bake for 30–35 minutes or until a skewer inserted into the centre comes out clean.

Remove from the oven and allow the cake to cool completely in the tin, then turn out onto a plate to serve. Serve in slices.

This cake will keep in an airtight container at room temperature for up to 3 days.

MINI COURGETTE CAKES WITH LIME ICING

MAKE 12 MINI CAKES

Equipment
12-cup muffin tin or silicone mould

For the courgette cakes
200g golden caster

175g plain flour

15g/1 tbsp baking powder

pinch of fine salt

3 eggs, beaten

110ml olive oil, plus extra for greasing

finely grated zest of 1 lemon

300g (trimmed weight) courgettes,
    coarsely grated

For the lime cream cheese icing
160g cream cheese

80g icing sugar

finely grated zest and juice of 1 lime,
    plus extra grated zest to decorate

Don't be put off by the savoury ingredients in this recipe, as these delicious mini cakes are truly magical. These bake especially well in a silicone mould as they have a tendency to stick otherwise.

Preheat the oven to 160°C fan/180°C/gas mark 4. Liberally grease the muffin tin/silicone mould with olive oil, then line the base of each cup with a small circle of baking paper.

For the cake, mix the dry ingredients (caster sugar, flour, baking powder and salt) together in a large mixing bowl, then mix the eggs, olive oil and lemon zest together in a separate mixing bowl.

Add the egg mixture into the dry mixture and whisk together until well combined. Finally, fold the courgettes through with a spatula until evenly mixed. Pour the batter into the greased muffin/mould cups, dividing it evenly and filling each one about three-quarters full.

Bake for about 25–30 minutes or until golden and a skewer inserted into the centre of each cake comes out clean.

Remove from the oven and leave the cakes to cool in the tin/mould for 15–20 minutes, then carefully remove to a wire rack and leave to cool completely before icing.

To make the icing, add all the ingredients to a medium bowl and beat together thoroughly with a wooden spoon until combined.

Spoon some icing on top of each cake and decorate with some extra lime zest sprinkled over. Serve and enjoy.

These cakes will keep in an airtight container at room temperature for up to 3 days.

Crowd

pleasers

A good dessert is a unifier of sorts – something that can break the barriers down amongst even the fussiest of eaters. If I'm making dessert for a group of people I'm not so familiar with, I like to make sure it's something of a crowd pleaser.

Even an awkward social gathering can become ever-so-sweet with the presence of a good pudding. My mum, in particular, always requests that I make classic crowd pleasers like crumbles, trifles or apple tarts for guests – she knows the power of a good dessert.

So, this chapter is dedicated to those recipes that can save the day and restore an evening.

TRIFLE

SERVES 10

Equipment

22 x 22 x 8cm (8½ x 8½ x 3¼in) serving dish

8–12 sponge fingers or the equivalent
   in sponge cake (cut into fingers)
sprinkles, to decorate

For the jelly

800ml water

135g caster sugar

300g fresh raspberries

350g fresh strawberries, hulled
   (halved if large)

7 'platinum-grade' gelatine leaves
   (I use Dr. Oetker)

juice of 1 lime or ½ lemon

For the custard

900ml double cream

300ml full-fat milk

225g caster sugar

3 eggs

5 egg yolks

3 heaped tbsp cornflour

pinch of Maldon or flaky salt

For the Chantilly cream

450ml double cream

1 tbsp caster sugar

pinch of Maldon or flaky salt

1 tsp vanilla extract (optional)

Quick Tip

The softened fruit left in the sieve can be
cooled and served with yogurt, if you like.

I absolutely believe that jelly has an important place in a trifle. During the summer months, it's a nice thing to make your jelly from scratch using fresh berries, but do know that frozen berries work well, too, when the winter needs brightening up. I'm also not against trifle fingers or slices of sponge cake as a base. I've tested making trifles with both home-made sponge fingers and shop-bought, and after the drenching and submerging of various liquids, creams and custards, I've come to realize that there is time better spent elsewhere. Like listening to the birds and drinking a cup of tea.

Make the jelly. In a large pan, add the water, sugar, 200g of the raspberries and 200g of the strawberries and stir well. Bring to a gentle simmer, then switch off the heat, cover and allow this to sit for 30 minutes.

In the meantime, soak the gelatine in ice-cold water until softened, then squeeze out the excess water and set aside ready to dissolve into the fruit mixture.

Strain the fruit liquid through a sieve into a jug (pressing the softened fruit very lightly to get a bit more flavour – see also *Quick Tip*), then pour the liquid back into the rinsed-out pan and return to the heat. When it's steaming, remove from the heat, add in the soaked gelatine, use a whisk and stir well until it has dissolved. Stir in the lime or lemon juice.

Allow the mixture to cool at room temperature until it is no longer warm to the touch – the jelly won't set at this point, don't worry.

Meanwhile, make the custard. In a blender or food processor, blitz everything together for a minute or two. Pour this mixture into a large pan and heat over a low-medium heat, whisking frequently, until it starts to thicken. It won't thicken dramatically but you will notice a difference in that it will stop swishing about as easily in the pan.

After 8–10 minutes at this pace, remove from the heat and pour into a heatproof container, then put a piece of baking paper directly on top of the custard (this stops a skin forming). Allow to cool before placing in the fridge for a minimum of 4 hours or until completely cold.

While the custard is chilling, start to assemble the trifle. Arrange the sponge fingers or sponge cake in the bottom of the serving dish of your choice along with the remaining raspberries and strawberries. Pour over the cool fruit jelly mix. Put this in the fridge until the jelly has set (approx. 4 hours).

While this is chilling, make the Chantilly cream. Lightly whip the cream with the sugar and salt until it looks just about whipped. Stir in the vanilla extract, if you like. The cream is now ready to be spooned on top of the custard.

To finish assembling the trifle, gently beat the chilled custard with a large spoon before spooning this over the set jelly mixture. Top with the Chantilly cream. Finish with sprinkles. Serve cold.

This trifle will keep, covered, in the fridge for 3–4 days.

SAFFRON RICE PUDDING

SERVES 6

Equipment

26cm (10½in) round casserole/ovenproof
pie dish (or ovenproof deep saucepan),
5cm (2in) deep

15g/1 tbsp unsalted butter

85g caster sugar

pinch of Maldon or flaky salt

1 tsp vanilla bean paste, or 1 vanilla pod
    split lengthways and seeds scraped out

110g pudding rice

400ml double cream

600ml full-fat milk, plus 2 tbsp for
    the saffron

large pinch of saffron strands

2 egg yolks

I served this saffron rice pudding as a dish at a pop-up with my friend Terri of Happy Endings, an ice-cream sandwich company in Mile End, London, in an effort to support Cook for Iran. I made kilos of it and we served it with a swirl of mango and milk soft-serve ice cream.

In this recipe, I don't cook the rice pudding with the saffron to start with as it dulls the flavour and saffron is so precious. Instead, I lightly pound the saffron in a pestle and mortar before adding it to the pot later on.

The egg yolks here give it a richness and depth without having to make a separate crème anglaise to stir in. This is a lot quicker, and when I suggested it online as a quick method, a lot of people reached out and said it's a method used by their grandmothers! Because it's only a small amount of egg yolk and the rice pudding is piping hot, it's definitely ok to do, however, if you prefer to avoid eggs, you can serve this without eggs and simply omit the step.

Preheat the oven to 130°C fan/150°C/gas mark 2.

Put the casserole dish or saucepan on the hob, add the butter and melt over a medium heat. When the butter starts to sizzle, stir in the sugar, salt and vanilla.

When the sugar starts to dissolve, pour in the rice and stir well, then follow this with 300ml of the cream and the 600ml of milk. Stir over a medium-low heat for 30 minutes – you don't need to stir religiously, just occasionally to keep it moving.

When the rice starts to float towards the top, pop the lid on and transfer it to the oven. Stir this every 20 minutes or so until the rice is cooked – typically this will take around 1–1¼ hours in the oven.

Gently pound the saffron with a pestle and mortar, stir in the remaining 2 tablespoons of milk and leave for 5 minutes. Set this aside for when the rice pudding is ready.

When the pudding is cooked, remove it from the oven. In a bowl, stir together the egg yolks with the infused saffron milk, then stir this through the cooked rice pudding. Pour in the remaining 100ml of double cream, stir well, then leave to stand for 5 minutes before serving.

BROWN BUTTER AND HONEY BAKED TART

SERVES 8

Equipment

20cm (8in) round tart tin, fluted or straight-edged; sturdy flat baking tray

For the pastry

125g plain flour, plus extra for dusting

40g icing sugar

pinch of fine salt

100g cold unsalted butter, cubed

2 egg yolks

1 egg, beaten, for the egg wash

For the filling

250ml double cream

200ml full-fat milk

60g golden caster sugar

4 egg yolks

30g honey

45g brown butter (made from approx. 60g unsalted butter – see *Quick Tip*)

3g/½ tsp Maldon or flaky salt

20g cornflour

Years ago, the brown butter and honey tart at the Marksman pub in Hackney was declared one of the best tarts in London (by me and the chefs at St. JOHN). So much so that we would often call ahead to reserve slices before a meal, and then when I left St. JOHN, we reserved three tarts for the table at the end as a must.

This is my nod to that tart, except this time it's baked high to caramelize the top, so it's a cross between a Parisian flan and a custard tart. A clear favourite and standout between my friends during the testing of this book.

To make the pastry, in a stand mixer fitted with the paddle attachment or a food processor or in a large bowl, combine the flour, icing sugar and salt. Mix well.

Add in the cold cubed butter and mix/pulse until the butter disappears and you have the texture of crumbs. If doing this by hand, rub into crumbs with your fingertips.

Add the egg yolks and mix quickly to form a dough. Tip this out onto your workbench and gently knead to bring it together nicely. Flatten into a disc, wrap tightly in clingfilm and chill in the fridge for 2 hours or until firm. Or freeze it at this stage for up to 3 months (defrost before use).

Line the tart tin with the pastry by rolling it out on a lightly floured work surface to the thickness of 3–4mm (⅛in) or a £1 coin, leaving an overhang. Chill in the fridge for 30–60 minutes, or wrap and freeze for up to 3 months (defrost before use).

Preheat the oven to 160°C fan/180°C/gas mark 4. Place the sturdy baking tray on a shelf/rack in the centre of the oven to preheat.

Continued overleaf →

Quick Tip

Make the brown butter by gently heating 60g of unsalted butter in a small pan over a low heat, then simmering until the butter has completely melted and starts to slowly brown, swirling the pan every so often. When it smells nutty and is frothing nicely, remove from the heat and pour into a heatproof bowl (this is important – if it's anything but, the bowl will melt). Leave to cool before use.

BROWN BUTTER AND HONEY BAKED TART

Prick the base of the pastry case all over, line the tin with baking paper and fill to the top with baking beans or dry rice/lentils. Put this on the preheated baking tray in the oven and bake for 20–25 minutes or until the edges are lightly golden.

Carefully remove the baking paper and beans/rice/lentils from the tin. Return the pastry case to the oven (on the baking tray) for 15–20 minutes, until the base is golden. If it starts to rise up, simply prick the base with a fork.

Brush the tart all over with the beaten egg, then return to the oven for 3–5 minutes to form a seal.

Remove from the oven and allow to cool slightly, then trim up the edges. Leave to cool completely before adding the filling.

When you are ready to fill and bake the tart, preheat the oven to 200°C fan/220°C/gas mark 7.

For the filling, warm 200ml of the cream and the milk with the sugar in a small pan until steaming.

In a heatproof bowl, gently whisk the egg yolks together with the honey, brown butter and salt. Whisk in the cornflour.

When the cream mixture is steaming, pour half of it over the yolk mixture and whisk well. Pour this back into the pan containing the remaining cream mixture. Heat over a medium heat and whisk constantly until it starts to thicken and bubble. After 2 minutes, remove from the heat and pour in the remaining 50ml of double cream and whisk well.

This mixture can now be poured into the tart shell and baked. It's best to use this mixture when it's still warm to ensure it bakes through and quickly.

Bake the tart for 15–20 minutes or until the top is bubbling and caramelized all over.

Remove from the oven and leave to cool in the tin, then carefully remove and serve in slices.

This tart is best eaten at room temperature on the day it is made, but it will keep, covered, in the fridge overnight.

APPLE TART

As pleasing and satisfying as this is to make, it also won the hearts of lots of people when I was asking for some feedback during my testing process. The pastry is crisp, moreish and slightly salty, and as the sliced apples bake, they release their scent into the inner edges of the pastry and sit prettily stacked on top of each other, creating a really beautiful dessert fit for friends who truly deserve it. Or it can be divvied up into portions and eaten on the go.

Continued overleaf →

'*A really beautiful dessert fit for friends who truly deserve it.*'

SERVES 8

Equipment

20cm (8in) sandwich cake tin, 3.5cm (1¼in) deep; sturdy flat baking tray

For the pastry

200g plain flour, plus extra for dusting

40g ground almonds

1 tbsp caster sugar

large pinch of fine salt

190g cold unsalted butter, cubed, plus extra (softened) for greasing

80g cream cheese

1 egg, beaten, for the egg wash

10g demerara sugar

For the apples

620g (approx. 5) Braeburn eating apples (or a firm red eating apple that bakes well without going mushy)

75g caster sugar

20ml rum

2 tbsp crab apple jelly, apricot jam or apple jelly, to glaze

icing sugar, for dusting (optional)

Make the pastry. In a large bowl, or the bowl of a stand mixer fitted with the paddle attachment, or a food processor, add the flour, almonds, sugar and salt and mix well. Add in the cold cubed butter and rub in with your fingertips or mix/pulse until it resembles loose breadcrumbs. Add in the cream cheese and mix briefly until a dough forms – it won't take very long. Don't be tempted to overwork the dough at this stage.

Tip the dough out onto your work surface and gently bring it together, before wrapping tightly in some baking paper or clingfilm and pressing to form a disc – this helps it to cool down evenly and quicker. Chill in the fridge for at least 2 hours until firm, or overnight.

Grease the sandwich tin liberally with softened butter and line the base with baking paper, then put this in the fridge while you roll out the dough.

Lightly flour the work surface, then gently knead the dough to make sure it's all evenly the same temperature. Roll out the dough to a rough circle about 4–5mm (¼in) thick – this will be folded over the apples so it needs to be a rough circle, almost galette-like in its assembly.

Transfer and press the dough into the prepared tin, making sure the dough is draping nicely over the edges of the tin.

Prepare the apples by coring, then thinly slicing them. It's best to do this quickly and to not submerge them in water even if they start to brown slightly. Toss them in a bowl with the sugar and rum.

Layer the apple slices into the pastry case – you don't need to be really precise or precious about it, but do bear in mind that the tart slices really nicely if it's layered up consistently. Fold the edges of the pastry over the apples, then refrigerate while you preheat the oven.

Preheat the oven to 170°C fan/190°C/gas mark 5. Place the sturdy baking tray on a shelf/rack in the middle of the oven to preheat.

Egg wash the pastry and sprinkle the demerara sugar on top. Place the tart on the preheated baking tray in the oven and bake for 40 minutes or until the pastry is deep golden.

Remove from the oven and allow the tart to cool slightly before removing it from the tin. If it cools too much, there's a risk that it will weld itself to the tin; if this happens, briefly warm it up again in the oven.

Glaze the tart with the jelly or jam by warming it up gently with a splash of water (in a small pan or microwave) and then brushing it over the apples. Dust the tart with icing sugar, if you like. Serve warm with crème fraîche, cream, custard, ice cream or on its own. That's a lot of options.

This tart will keep in an airtight container in the fridge for up to 2 days. Eat cold or reheat in a hot oven to enjoy.

CHOCOLATE AND HAZELNUT CARAMEL TART

SERVES 8

Equipment

20cm (8in) round tart tin, 3.5cm (1¼in) deep, fluted or straight-edged; sturdy flat baking tray; rimmed baking tray

For the pastry

100g plain flour

1g/large pinch of Maldon or flaky salt

20g cocoa powder

40g icing sugar

80g cold unsalted butter, cubed, plus extra (softened) for greasing

2 egg yolks

For the chocolate ganache

250ml double cream

30g honey

3g/½ tsp Maldon or flaky salt

60g milk chocolate (40–55 per cent cocoa solids), roughly chopped

70g dark chocolate (70 per cent cocoa solids), roughly chopped

For the hazelnut topping

100g blanched whole hazelnuts

100g caster sugar

15g/1 tbsp unsalted butter

100ml double cream

pinch of Maldon or flaky salt

This tart is unbelievably fun to put together and the result is really impressive. The hazelnuts sit on top of the silk-like ganache like golden jewels, and texturally, it keeps you coming back for more. It's one of those desserts that ticks every box, for me and most people I like anyway.

Because of the nature of this tart, with this dough you want a thicker edge that doesn't need to be too neatly lined, as you are going to press the pastry into the tin directly after it's made without chilling it first.

Line the base of the tart tin with a circle of baking paper and lightly butter the sides of the tin, then put this in the fridge.

Make the pastry. In a large bowl or the bowl of a stand mixer or food processor, mix together the flour, salt, cocoa powder and icing sugar. Add the cold cubed butter and mix to form breadcrumbs, either with your fingertips, the paddle attachment or pulsed in the food processor. Add the egg yolks in one go and mix briefly to form a dough. Tip this onto your work surface and knead briefly to form a homogeneous dough. Press this pastry into the chilled lined tin, using both thumbs to get it nicely around and up the edges and over the base in an even layer. Refrigerate for 2 hours or until firm.

Preheat the oven to 160°C fan/180°C/gas mark 4. Place the sturdy flat baking tray on a shelf/rack in the centre of the oven to preheat.

Blind-bake the pastry. Line the pastry case with a sheet of baking paper and fill to the top with baking beans or dried rice/lentils. Put this on the preheated baking tray in the oven and bake for 20–25 minutes or until the edges are lightly golden. Carefully remove the baking paper and beans, then return to the oven (on the baking tray) for 15–20 minutes until fully cooked. Remove from the oven and allow to cool completely in the tin.

Make the ganache. In a small saucepan, warm the cream with the honey and salt until steaming. Place all the chopped chocolate into a heatproof bowl. Pour the warmed cream over the chocolate and leave to sit for 30 seconds. Using a whisk, stir the mixture from the very middle, gently and slowly moving it to the outer edges until a smooth ganache forms.

Continued overleaf →

CHOCOLATE AND HAZELNUT
CARAMEL TART *continued*

Pour the ganache into the tart shell and leave it to set at room temperature, it should take around 3 hours. If it's a particularly warm day or it needs a bit of a nudge, pop it into the fridge until it firms up.

In the meantime, roast the hazelnuts for the topping (this will give a better texture to the tart). Preheat the oven to 150°C fan/170°C/gas mark 3½. Put the hazelnuts on the rimmed baking tray in a single layer and roast for 13–15 minutes until golden brown, keeping an eye on them. Remove from the oven and set aside.

To finish the hazelnut topping, in a saucepan, heat the sugar over a medium heat, gently swirling it in the pan (use a spatula to move it gently if it needs a bit of help distributing the heat if it's not caramelizing evenly) and keeping an eye on it. Once it's a golden, rich, deep colour, add the butter and stir well to combine. Stir in the cream and heat gently until a caramel sauce forms. Stir in the roasted whole hazelnuts and the salt.

Remove from the heat and let this cool temporarily so it's not scalding hot to melt the ganache. Once cool enough, tip the hazelnut caramel onto the set ganache in an even layer. Leave this to set for 30 minutes before serving, then serve as it is or with a dollop of crème fraîche.

This tart is best eaten on the day it is made. Leftovers will keep in an airtight container in the fridge for up to 2 days, but the texture will soften.

'It's one of those desserts that ticks every box.'

RAV'S CREAM CRUMBLE

SERVES 10

Equipment

28 x 22cm (11 x 8½in) rectangular pie tin sturdy rimmed baking tray

For the fruit

650g apples (I use a mix of Bramley, Braeburn and Pink Lady apples), peeled, cored and chopped into 1–2cm (½–¾in) pieces

125g fresh blackberries

130g caster sugar

1 vanilla pod, halved lengthways and seeds scraped out, or 1 tsp vanilla bean paste (optional)

For the crumble

300g plain flour

2g/scant ½ tsp Maldon or flaky salt

150g caster sugar

150g cold unsalted butter, cubed

4–5 tbsp double cream

This is an all-in-one crumble recipe. If you've followed my work, you've probably heard me say that I like cooking my fruit and topping separately to maximize crunch and the eating experience. However, now that I'm not cooking in restaurants, I've had to adjust the way I cook and bake, no longer with the mentality that I've got to think about service, longevity and hundreds of portions.

I wanted to make a crumble that wasn't claggy, but had a touch of chew and a good crunch. Through a lot of crumble conversations, the general consensus was that fruit is good, it should contrast to the buttery topping, but that the main star of the show is, in fact, the crumble, which I wholeheartedly agree with. The cream addition here lightens it up and allows for a really beautiful bake with enough crisp and just the right proportion of chew.

I've used a mix of apples and blackberries here, but you can change that according to what's available – rhubarb and apple is another of my favourite combinations.

Preheat the oven to 175°C fan/195°C/gas mark 5½.

Combine the chopped apples, the blackberries, sugar and vanilla (if using) in the casserole dish and mix well using your hands.

Make the crumble. In a large bowl, mix together the flour, salt and sugar. Add the cold cubed butter and use your fingertips to breadcrumb the butter into the flour mix. Use a light touch and don't worry if there are a few lumps, it's good if the breadcrumbs are slightly irregular as it makes for a really nice overall bake with pockets of texture.

Once you've achieved this, add the cream by dotting the tablespoons around the top of the bowl so you don't add it all in one place. Lightly and evenly mix this into the crumbed mixture – it won't feel like a lot but that's ok.

Use your hands to pile the crumble mixture onto the prepared fruit in one layer. There's no need to pat it down, it will cook well if it's uneven on top and rough. Place the dish on the rimmed baking tray – this will catch any of the fruit juices that bubble over.

Bake for 45 minutes or until golden all over with some of the fruit filling bubbling around the sides.

Remove from the oven and allow to cool for 10 minutes before serving, jugs of custard and cream at the ready.

This crumble is best served hot, but it will keep in an airtight container in the fridge for up to 3 days. Reheat in a hot oven until piping hot before serving. You can, of course, eat it cold, but I prefer it hot.

STICKY DATE AND MALT PUDDING

SERVES 3–4

Equipment
small ovenproof pie/baking dish,
about 18 x 13.5 x 5cm (7 x 5¼ x 2in)

For the sponge
50g unsalted butter, at room temperature
100g date molasses
30g soft dark brown sugar
50ml full-fat milk
1 egg, beaten
150g plain flour
25g malt powder
1 tsp baking powder
½ tsp bicarbonate of soda
pinch of fine salt
½ tsp ground ginger

For the sauce
30g soft dark brown sugar
100ml double cream
20g unsalted butter
pinch of Maldon or flaky salt

I get a lot of enquiries about sticky toffee pudding. It can go wrong quite quickly and people often report a dense almost raw middle that sometimes occurs. I have also had this in the past and, after teaching a few sticky toffee pudding classes, I've figured out that it is related to the amount of water that is left over once the dates are heated and the reaction of the bicarbonate of soda.

Therefore, I wanted to create a pudding that has the appeal of a sticky toffee pudding without the variables. I've done this by using date molasses and it works like a dream. It means there's less mess and the whole thing can be made while your friends are distracting you.

Preheat the oven to 165°C fan/185°C/gas mark 4½.

Make the sponge. In a bowl, beat the butter, date molasses and brown sugar together until combined. Scrape down the sides of the bowl and mix in the milk. Add the egg and mix well.

In a separate bowl, stir together the flour, malt powder, baking powder, bicarbonate of soda, salt and ginger. Add the dry ingredients to the butter mixture and mix until a smooth batter forms. Pour into the ovenproof pie/baking dish (there's no need to grease the dish first) and spread evenly.

Bake for 28–30 minutes or until a skewer inserted into the centre comes out clean.

Remove from the oven and set aside to cool for 10 minutes.

Make the sauce. Heat all the sauce ingredients together in a saucepan over a medium heat, stirring occasionally, until combined and the sauce is about to boil, then remove from the heat.

Serve the sponge pudding warm with the hot sauce spooned over.

Leftovers will keep in an airtight container in the fridge for up to 3 days. Reheat in a moderate oven for 10–15 minutes or microwave on medium power until steaming before eating.

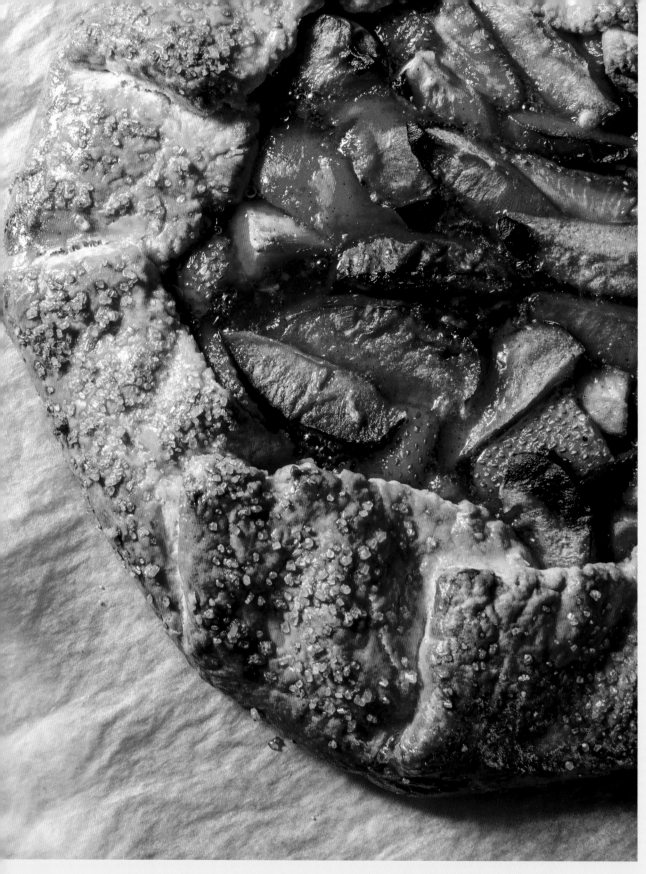

SUMMER FRUIT GALETTE

**MAKES 1 X 25CM (10IN)
GALETTE; SERVES 10**

Vary the fruit as you please with this galette, depending on the season, and adjust for sweetness if you are using something tart like rhubarb or apples.

Equipment
large rimmed baking tray

For the pastry
30g light rye flour

180g plain flour, plus extra for dusting

pinch of Maldon or flaky salt

2 tbsp caster sugar

150g unsalted butter, at room
    temperature

180g cream cheese

For the fruit mixture
200g fresh strawberries

300g fresh plums

150g caster sugar

20g cornflour

finely grated zest and juice of ½ lemon

1 tsp vanilla extract

To finish
1 egg, beaten with a pinch of fine salt,
    for the egg wash

demerara sugar, for sprinkling

Make the pastry. In a large bowl, mix together both flours, the salt and sugar. Set aside.

In another large bowl, mix together the butter and cream cheese until homogeneous. Tip in the dry ingredients and mix well, either using a large wooden spoon or your fingertips. Alternatively, pulse in a food processor or mix in the bowl of a stand mixer fitted with the paddle attachment. The dough should come together quite quickly.

As soon as it forms a dough, tip it onto a sheet of baking paper or clingfilm, knead it gently and shape into a disc, then wrap tightly before chilling in the fridge for 2 hours or until firm (or overnight).

For the fruit mixture, halve the strawberries and cut the plums into quarters, removing the stones. Place the fruit in a bowl and toss with the sugar, cornflour, lemon zest and juice and vanilla. Set aside for a maximum of 30 minutes before use.

When you are ready to assemble the galette, preheat the oven to 165°C fan/185°C/gas mark 4½. Line the baking tray with baking paper (using a rimmed baking tray helps here in case of any leaks).

On a lightly floured surface, gently knead the pastry briefly before rolling it out to a round, about 30cm (12in) in diameter and 5mm (¼in) thick, then transfer this to the prepared baking tray.

Tip the fruit mixture into the middle of the pastry round, leaving a 5cm (2in) border all around the edge. Fold this border of pastry over the fruit filling to overlap/cover the edges of the filling all the way round (the fruit filling will be left uncovered in the centre). Egg wash the pastry edges and then sprinkle liberally with demerara sugar.

Bake for 1¼ hours or until the pastry edges are golden and the fruit is bubbling.

Remove from the oven and allow to cool slightly on the baking tray, then slide the galette onto a serving board/plate and serve warm or cold in slices. Serve with pouring cream, custard or ice cream.

Leftovers will keep in an airtight container in the fridge for up to 2 days.

LIGHT-AS-AIR CHOCOLATE, CHERRY AND PISTACHIO ROULADE

SERVES 8

A roulade for pretty much any occasion, this isn't the type of sheet sponge that dries out quickly or breaks as you roll it. It's really 'user-friendly' and can be frozen ahead of time, too (see *Quick Tip*).

Equipment

38 x 28cm (15 x 11in) Swiss roll-type tin or shallow (rimmed) baking tin/tray; a second rimmed baking tray

For the chocolate sponge

60g plain flour

1 tbsp cocoa powder, plus extra for dusting

1 tsp baking powder

¼ tsp fine salt

4 eggs, separated

¼ tsp cream of tartar

100g caster sugar

70ml neutral oil, such as sunflower, vegetable or rapeseed oil, plus extra for greasing

3 tbsp full-fat milk

For the filling

250ml double cream

30g ready-made pistachio cream or pistachio butter

pinch of Maldon or flaky salt

1 tbsp caster sugar

15g/1 tbsp shelled pistachios, roughly chopped

80g (drained weight) canned pitted cherries, drained

For the coating/glaze

180ml double cream

40g apricot jam

15ml neutral oil, such as sunflower, vegetable or rapeseed oil

100g dark chocolate (70 per cent cocoa solids), chopped

Preheat the oven to 160°C fan/180°C/gas mark 4. Grease and line the base and sides of the baking tin/tray with baking paper.

Make the chocolate sponge. In a medium bowl, mix together the flour, cocoa powder, baking powder and salt. Set aside.

In a large clean bowl, using an electric handheld whisk (or in the bowl of a stand mixer with the whisk attachment), whisk the egg whites with the cream of tartar until frothy. Add half of the caster sugar into the egg whites and continue to whisk on a medium speed until it looks shiny and meringue-like.

In a separate large bowl, whisk the egg yolks with the remaining caster sugar until combined, then whisk in the oil and milk. Fold in the dry ingredients using the whisk, until combined, then fold the meringue into this mixture in thirds until a homogeneous mix comes together. Spoon this into the prepared baking tin/tray and spread evenly.

Bake for 10–12 minutes or until the sponge is set but is still soft and springy to touch – it shouldn't stick to your fingers at all.

Remove from the oven and allow the sponge to cool completely in the tin/tray.

For the filling, in a bowl, whip together the double cream, pistachio cream/butter, salt and caster sugar until the mixture forms soft peaks and just about holds together. When spreading this on the roulade, it will come together even more, so it's better to slightly under-whip than over-whip here.

Continued overleaf →

LIGHT-AS-AIR CHOCOLATE, CHERRY AND PISTACHIO ROULADE *continued*

To assemble the roulade, take two large sheets of baking paper, each 5cm (2in) wider than the width and 10cm (4in) longer than the length of the baked sponge. The paper will help you to roll up the roulade.

Lay one of these sheets of baking paper on the work surface and invert the cooked sponge onto it, then peel off and discard the lining paper – this will be the outside of the roulade, so then (with the help of the paper underneath) carefully flip the sponge over onto the other sheet of paper, so the baked-side is uppermost. Remove the sheet of paper now on top and use it to line a small tray, then set aside. Using the sheet of paper underneath the roulade to help you, starting from a long edge, roll up the roulade first without the filling (and with the paper inside) and leave this for 5 minutes, then unroll.

Spread the pistachio cream filling evenly over the sponge, leaving a 5cm (2in) border along one long edge of the sponge – this is so the filling doesn't spill out of the roulade when you roll it up. Sprinkle over the pistachios and then line up the cherries on the opposite long edge in a single line (on the cream filling). Tightly roll up the roulade from this long edge (nearest to the cherries), using the paper again to help you to roll it tightly (this time keeping the paper on the outside of the roulade; once the roulade is rolled-up, the paper can be discarded).

Transfer the roulade to the lined small tray, placing it seam-side down, then refrigerate for 45–60 minutes before coating with the glaze (see also *Quick Tip*).

Meanwhile, make the coating/glaze. Heat the cream, apricot jam and oil together in a pan over a medium heat until steaming. Remove from the heat, then stir in the chopped chocolate until melted and combined. Set aside to cool until it is no longer hot to touch (it should be pourable but not hot).

Transfer the chilled roulade (keeping it seam-side down) to a wire rack with a rimmed baking tray underneath (to catch any drips). Pour the chocolate glaze evenly over the roulade to coat it. Use a spatula to lift the roulade and gently turn it on the rack ever so slightly so you can coat the underneath. Place the glazed roulade back on the lined tray and refrigerate for 10 minutes or so before serving.

Transfer the roulade to a serving board/platter, dust with a little cocoa powder and then serve in slices.

Leftover roulade will keep in an airtight container in the fridge for up to 3 days.

Quick Tip

Once the roulade has been filled, rolled-up and chilled, it can be wrapped tightly in clingfilm and frozen for up to 1 month. Make the coating/glaze as above, then pour this over the frozen roulade. Leave the glazed roulade to defrost fully before serving as above.

CLASSIC CREAM BIRTHDAY CAKE

MAKES 1 LARGE BIRTHDAY CAKE (2 LAYERS); SERVES 10–12

This cake is light, airy and a joy to eat. It can be made as it is for a birthday or celebration, or simply cut into sandwich-style slices and individually wrapped to be given to friends. Biji (my Grandma) is a huge fan of this cake, because she doesn't have teeth.

Equipment

2 x 28 x 18 x 5cm (11 x 7 x 2in) baking/cake tins

unsalted butter, for greasing

For the cake

5 eggs

220g caster sugar

220g plain flour

3 tsp baking powder

large pinch of fine salt

80ml neutral oil, such as sunflower, vegetable or rapeseed oil

green food colouring gel

finely grated zest of 1 lime

orange food colouring gel

finely grated zest of 1 orange

For the syrup

50g caster sugar

70ml water

juice of ½ lemon

For the filling

300ml double cream

1 tbsp caster sugar

a pinch of Maldon or flaky salt

200g jam of your choice

icing sugar, for dusting

Preheat the oven to 160°C fan/180°C/gas mark 4. Lightly grease the two baking/cake tins with butter and line with baking paper.

For the cake, in the bowl of a stand mixer with the whisk attachment, or in a large bowl using an electric handheld whisk, whisk the eggs on a medium speed for a few minutes. Add the sugar and continue to whisk on a medium speed for 15–18 minutes or until the mixture is thick and at the 'ribbon stage' – this is when the whisk is lifted out of the bowl and some of the mix drizzled on top holds itself and holds its shape for a few seconds. Pour this mixture into a large clean bowl.

In a separate bowl, stir together the flour, baking powder and salt. Alternately, sift and fold the flour mix into the whisked egg and sugar mixture in thirds, drizzling a third of the oil in after each addition of flour. Fold gently after each addition, being careful not to overmix.

Divide the cake batter in half – place half in another bowl and leave the rest in the first bowl. Colour one portion of cake batter with green food colouring (add the food colouring gel with a cocktail stick or toothpick to the depth of colour you like), adding the lime zest and folding both in gently until evenly combined, then colour the other portion with orange food colouring, adding the orange zest and folding both in gently. Pour each coloured batter into one of the prepared tins and spread it level.

Bake for 18–20 minutes or until a skewer inserted into the centre of each cake comes out clean.

Continued overleaf →

CLASSIC CREAM BIRTHDAY CAKE *continued*

Remove from the oven and allow the cakes to cool in the tins for 20 minutes before turning them out onto wire racks to cool completely.

Meanwhile, make the syrup. In a small saucepan, heat the sugar, water and lemon juice together over a medium until the sugar has dissolved, then simmer for 2 minutes. Remove from the heat and leave to cool until warm (use it warm).

For the filling, in a bowl, lightly whip the cream, sugar and salt together until soft peaks form.

To assemble the cake, brush the warm syrup over each sponge layer and set aside for 5 minutes.

Place one sponge on a serving board/platter and spread the jam evenly over the sponge. Top with the whipped cream in an even layer. Place the second sponge on top (see *Quick Tip*). Chill the cake in the fridge for 20 minutes before serving and slicing. Dust the top with icing sugar just before serving.

This cake will keep in an airtight container in the fridge for up to 3 days.

Quick Tip

If you would also like to cover the top of the cake with cream, simply double the ingredient quantities of the cream mixture for the filling, then use half for sandwiching the cakes together and the rest for the top of the cake. Decorate with extra citrus zest and some sprinkles.

CHURROS

MAKES 10 LARGE CHURROS

Equipment

deep-fat fryer, or large, deep, heavy-based saucepan

For the cinnamon sugar

100g caster sugar

2 tsp ground cinnamon

For the churros

250ml water

90g unsalted butter

20g caster sugar

¼ tsp fine salt

140g plain flour

3 eggs

approx. 1.5 litres vegetable or sunflower oil, for deep-frying

For the chocolate dipping sauce

(*optional*)

160g dark chocolate (70 per cent cocoa solids), roughly chopped

180ml water

2 tbsp caster sugar

If you know me, you'll know I'm a sucker for deep-fried food, I can't resist it. If I'm ever at a market and I spot churros, the likelihood of me buying some is very high. I love their texture, crisp on the outside and fluffy and light on the inside.

These churros are great served on their own, dusted in cinnamon sugar, or with the chocolate dipping sauce. The method for making the batter is the same as for choux pastry.

Make the cinnamon sugar by simply combining the sugar and cinnamon in a bowl. Set aside.

Make the churros mixture. In a large saucepan, combine the water, butter, sugar and salt and bring to a rolling boil (this is important), then reduce the heat slightly and add the flour in one go. Use a sturdy wooden or heatproof spoon and mix this vigorously until the mixture comes together and comes away from the sides of the pan.

Stir over a medium heat for a few minutes, then remove from the heat and transfer to a large heatproof bowl or the bowl of a stand mixer. Leave to cool for about 15 minutes before you start adding the eggs. In a separate bowl, whisk the eggs together.

Heat the oil in the deep-fat fryer or large, deep saucepan over a medium-low heat until it's 160°C/320°F or until a cube of bread browns in about 45 seconds.

Meanwhile, finish the churros mixture. Using an electric handheld whisk or the paddle attachment (if using a stand mixer), start adding the whisked eggs to the cooled choux mixture in the bowl, mixing well after each addition. You are looking for the mixture to turn glossy, smooth and to be at 'dropping consistency' (when you lift the mixture out of the bowl on a spoon and give it a very gentle nudge, it should drop from the spoon, it shouldn't run off the spoon or cling to it). You may not need to add all the beaten eggs, so add them gradually and check the consistency regularly.

Continued overleaf →

Spoon the mixture into a piping bag fitted with a star-shaped nozzle (I use a 1M star-shaped nozzle). Pipe long strips (each about 12cm/4½in long) of the churro batter directly into the hot oil, using a pair of scissors to chop the end off the batter by the piping nozzle to get a clean edge. Deep-fry 2–3 at a time for about 5–6 minutes per batch, turning occasionally.

Lift the cooked churros out of the oil using a slotted spoon or the basket of the deep-fat fryer and drain on kitchen paper. Repeat with the remaining churros batter, to make about 10 churros in total, remembering to bring the oil back up to temperature before frying each batch.

Allow each batch of churros to cool for a few minutes before dusting in the cinnamon sugar. Serve warm, on their own or with the warm chocolate dipping sauce (see below). Churros are best eaten warm as soon as they are made (or they can be enjoyed cold, within 2 hours of making).

To make the chocolate dipping sauce (if using), heat the chocolate, water and sugar together in a medium saucepan over a medium heat, stirring frequently until the chocolate has melted. Keep stirring with a whisk until a smooth sauce forms. Remove from the heat, pour into small heatproof bowls and serve immediately with the churros.

'Crisp on the outside and fluffy and light on the inside.'

STRAWBERRY AND CLOTTED CREAM PARIS-BREST

MAKES 5 PARIS-BREST;
EACH ONE SERVES 2

These are wonderful in the summer at the height of the strawberry season. Make these for friends to enjoy in the afternoon or to serve at the end of a summer barbecue.

Equipment
large flat baking tray

1 x quantity of craquelin (see Coffee Choux recipe on page 39)
1 x quantity of choux pastry (see Coffee Choux recipe on page 39)

For the clotted cream mousseline
400ml full-fat milk
120g caster sugar
large pinch of Maldon or flaky salt
5 egg yolks
50g cornflour
150g clotted cream
100g unsalted butter, softened

For the strawberries
200g fresh strawberries, hulled and quartered
20g golden caster sugar
juice of ¼ lemon

icing sugar, for dusting

First, make the clotted cream mousseline. Make a crème pâtissière. In a medium saucepan, heat the milk with half the sugar and the salt over a medium heat until steaming. In a heatproof bowl, whisk the egg yolks with the remaining sugar and the cornflour until smooth and combined.

When the milk is steaming, gradually pour it over the egg yolk mixture and whisk well. Return to the pan and whisk vigorously over a medium heat until thick and bubbling, about 4–5 minutes. Remove from the heat.

Place the clotted cream in a separate heatproof bowl. Pour the hot crème pâtissière directly over the clotted cream and stir with a whisk to combine, then either use a stick blender or transfer the mixture to a blender or food processor and blitz for a few minutes – this is important to properly emulsify the additional fats in the crème pâtissière. Pour the mixture into a clean heatproof container, then place a sheet of greaseproof paper or clingfilm directly on the surface (to prevent a skin forming). Leave to cool, then chill in the fridge for at least 4 hours or overnight (see *Quick Tips*).

Meanwhile, make the craquelin dough following the instructions on page 39. Tip the dough out onto a sheet of baking paper, top with another sheet of baking paper, then roll out to 3–4mm (⅛–¼in) thickness. Put this on a tray and chill in the fridge for 1 hour or until set like a sheet of biscuit.

In the meantime, make the choux pastry following the instructions on pages 39–40.

Continued overleaf →

STRAWBERRY AND CLOTTED CREAM PARIS-BREST *continued*

Preheat the oven to 200°C fan/220°C/gas mark 7. Line the large baking tray with baking paper.

Fit a piping bag with a star-shaped nozzle (I use a 1cm/½in star-shaped nozzle) and fill the bag with the choux pastry. Take the lined baking tray. You can either draw a guide on the paper to pipe over, or you can freestyle-pipe instead. If drawing a guide, take two round biscuit cutters (one 8cm/3¼in and the other 3cm/1¼in) and use them to draw each doughnut shape on the paper (by putting the smaller cutter inside the larger one), making sure you leave enough space between the rings on the paper so that the choux can grow and expand in the oven during baking. Mark out five rings in total. Turn the paper over on the baking tray (so the guide marks are on the underside but are still visible through the paper) and thickly pipe the choux pastry over the ring shapes.

Cut out five rings of craquelin the same size as the choux rings (using the same cutters) and place one of these directly on top of each piped choux ring. Any scraps of craquelin can be re-rolled or wrapped in clingfilm and frozen for up to 1 month (defrost before use).

Bake for 20 minutes, but do not open the door! Lower the oven temperature to 170°C fan/190°C/gas mark 5 and bake for a further 15–20 minutes. To judge whether the choux is baked, gently lift one ring up and feel if it is light or heavy. If the choux feels heavy in any way, it will need a little longer in the oven to dry out, but if it feels light to touch, hollow and crisp, then it is ready.

Remove from the oven, then transfer the choux rings to a wire rack and leave to cool completely. Once cool, slice each choux ring horizontally in half (see *Quick Tips*).

Prepare the strawberries 20 minutes before assembling the Paris-Brest. In a small bowl, mix together the strawberries, sugar and lemon juice. Set aside.

When you are ready to assemble, place the chilled mousseline in the bowl of a stand mixer with the whisk attachment and whip on a medium speed, add the butter and continue to whip until thick and glossy. Transfer it to a piping bag fitted with a star-shaped nozzle (I use an 8mm/⅜in nozzle).

To assemble the Paris-Brest, remove the top half of each choux ring, then pipe the mousseline in a continuous ring/circle (or in small spirals/star shapes) inside each bottom half. Top generously with some strawberries. Place the top choux ring halves on top, then dust with icing sugar. Eat and enjoy!

The finished Paris-Brest should be eaten immediately or placed in the fridge for eating later, but they are best eaten on the day they are filled.

Quick Tips

The chilled mousseline will keep in an airtight container in the fridge for up to 3 days. When whipping this mixture, keep an eye on it to ensure it doesn't split. Once whipped, pipe or use it immediately.

The baked choux rings can be cooled completely and frozen in an airtight container for up to 1 month. To use, simply defrost the choux rings at room temperature, then place on a lined baking tray and refresh in a moderate oven (160°C fan/180°C/gas mark 4) for 5–6 minutes or until they have heated through, then allow to cool before using as directed (the choux will crisp up again as it cools).

Instead of using mousseline as the filling, you can also try this with Chantilly cream (see page 72 for the recipe).

APPLE STRUDEL

SERVES 8–10

Equipment
large flat baking tray

For the pastry
150g plain flour, plus extra for dusting

75g strong white flour

¼ tsp fine salt

2 tsp caster sugar

150ml water

60g unsalted butter, melted and cooled

neutral oil, for greasing

For the filling
330g (unprepped weight) apples (I use a
    mix of Braeburn and Bramley)

40g soft light brown sugar

40g caster sugar

40g rum-soaked raisins (see *Quick Tip* on
    page 187)

½ tsp ground cinnamon

pinch of Maldon or flaky salt

To assemble and finish
70g unsalted butter or ghee, melted and
    cooled

20g dried breadcrumbs (white, brown or
    sourdough work well)

2 tbsp demerara sugar

icing sugar, for dusting (optional)

It might feel daunting making your own pastry for a strudel, but it is a really satisfying process. The dough is more robust than you think, and the more you make this, the better and more confident you will become.

Make the pastry. In the bowl of a stand mixer, mix together both flours, the salt and caster sugar. Add in the water and melted butter. Mix using the dough hook until a smooth dough forms (it will come together quickly). Take a large bowl and grease it with oil. Shape the dough into a ball and place it into the oiled bowl, then cover with a damp tea towel and leave to rest at room temperature for 2 hours.

To prepare the sheet of dough you will need to have the filling ready and the butter or ghee melted and cooled ready for brushing. If you can, ask a friend to help you with this if it's your first time.

Make the filling. Peel, halve and core the apples. Place each half, cored-side down, on a chopping board. Slice each half into thin slices, each about 2–3mm (1⁄16–1⁄8in) thick. In a bowl, toss the sliced apples with both sugars, the rum-soaked raisins, cinnamon and salt. Set aside.

Preheat the oven to 160°C fan/180°C/gas mark 4. Line the baking tray with baking paper.

Take a regular-sized clean tea towel and place it on the work surface. Very lightly dust it with flour. Take the rested dough and gently start to roll it out into a rectangle on the tea towel. When it reaches the thickness of 5mm (¼in), start using your fingers and palms to gently work the pastry out gently – it will stretch. When the pastry is transparent or as thin as you can get it (don't worry if there are a few holes in the sheet of pastry, just be wary of them when you are brushing with melted butter/ghee so it doesn't cause the pastry to stick), brush it with some of the melted butter/ghee.

Sprinkle the breadcrumbs evenly over the prepared pastry. Follow with the apple filling, spreading it evenly over the pastry, but leaving a border (about a quarter of the pastry) along one long side of the pastry free from filling. You'll be rolling it up from a long side (horizontally) starting from the side with the filling.

Use the tea towel to help you roll up the pastry to enclose the filling (like a Swiss roll), using the bare border of the pastry to help tuck the ends in and finish the strudel to prevent leakage as it bakes. Use the tea towel to help ease the strudel onto the lined baking tray, seam-side down. Brush it liberally with the remaining melted butter/ghee, then sprinkle over the demerara sugar.

Bake for 50 minutes–1¼ hours until golden all over.

Remove from the oven and allow to cool slightly on the baking tray, then slide the strudel onto a serving board/platter and dust with a little icing sugar, if you wish. Serve warm or cold in slices, and with your choice of pouring cream, custard or ice cream.

Leftovers will keep in an airtight container in the fridge for up to 2 days.

LEMON CREAM CAKE

This is another type of cake that my Biji wants on repeat – it's simple, full of cream and a bit lemony (and hard to resist!).

Equipment
2 x 15cm (6in) sandwich cake tins

For the cake
4 eggs

180g caster sugar

100g unsalted butter, melted, plus extra (softened) for greasing

50ml neutral oil, such as sunflower, vegetable or rapeseed oil

50g soured cream or natural yogurt

pinch of fine salt

finely grated zest of 1 lemon

200g plain flour

2½ tsp baking powder

For the syrup
120g caster sugar

100ml water

juice of 3 lemons

To finish
180ml double cream

icing sugar, for dusting

Preheat the oven to 160°C fan/180°C/gas mark 4. Lightly grease and line the cake tins with baking paper.

For the cake, in a large bowl, whisk together the eggs and sugar until combined, then whisk in the melted butter, oil, soured cream or yogurt, salt and lemon zest.

In a separate bowl, mix together the flour and baking powder. Add this to the egg mixture and mix well.

Divide the batter evenly between the two prepared cake tins and spread it level.

Bake for 25–30 minutes or until a skewer inserted into the centre of each cake comes out clean.

While the cakes are baking, make the syrup. Heat the sugar and water together in a small pan over a medium heat, stirring until the sugar has dissolved, then add the lemon juice and heat until the syrup is just about to boil. Remove from the heat and cool until warm before using.

Remove the cakes from the oven and allow to cool in the tins for 20 minutes. Prick the surface of each cake all over with a cocktail stick or fine skewer, then evenly pour over the warm syrup. Leave the cakes to sit for 4 hours before removing them from the tins, ready to fill.

To finish, whip the cream in a bowl until soft peaks form. Trim the tops off the cakes to neaten them, if needed, then sandwich them together with the whipped cream. Dust the top of the cake with icing sugar and serve in slices.

This cake will keep in an airtight container in the fridge for up to 3 days.

TIRAMISU

SERVES 10–12

Equipment

28 x 18 x 5cm (11 x 7 x 2in) baking tin

350ml brewed espresso, cooled to room temperature

50ml rum, Marsala or brandy

30 savoiardi (ladyfingers) or sponge fingers

4 egg yolks

160g caster sugar

500g good-quality Italian mascarpone cheese, at room temperature

180ml double cream

pinch of Maldon or flaky salt

30g dark chocolate (70 per cent cocoa solids), for grating

One of my biggest requests is for tiramisu. In my first book, I included a note about how to make a tiramisu, which, if it goes wrong, can be churned into an ice cream. I gave instructions on how to make your own sponge fingers, but now looking back, the whole recipe is quite cheffy. So I wanted to write a recipe for a simpler, easier-to-put-together recipe. I also use shop-bought sponge fingers now for consistency and to lower stress levels. Use the best quality eggs, as fresh as possible, as they're not cooked for this recipe... but you will be ok!!

The tiramisu needs to be chilled for at least 4 hours before serving, but it's even better if you can make it the day before you wish to serve, and chill it overnight.

Mix the espresso with 20ml of the booze of your choice in a shallow casserole dish. Briefly dip each sponge finger into the espresso mixture on both sides, then place into the bottom of the baking tin, covering the base – it will take about 15 sponge fingers to do this (don't dip the remaining sponge fingers just yet). Set aside.

In the bowl of a stand mixer with the whisk attachment, or in a bowl with an electric handheld whisk, whisk the egg yolks and sugar together until pale, thick and fluffy, about 10–15 minutes. Slowly beat in the mascarpone until there are no lumps. It should still be thick.

In a separate bowl, gently whip the cream with the remaining 30ml of booze and the salt until soft peaks form. Fold this through the mascarpone mixture to combine.

Spoon half of the mascarpone mixture over the layer of dipped sponge fingers in the tin. Dip the rest of the sponge fingers in the remaining espresso mixture and place them over the mascarpone in a single layer. Top with the remaining mascarpone mixture to cover the sponge fingers, spreading it level.

Cover and refrigerate for at least 4 hours or preferably overnight.

Just before serving, grate the chocolate all over the top of the dessert, then tuck in and enjoy.

Leftovers will keep in an airtight container in the fridge for up to 2 days.

CLASSIC CHOCOLATE MOUSSE

SERVES 10

Equipment
large serving dish or bowl

2 'platinum-grade' gelatine leaves
   (I use Dr. Oetker)

510ml double cream

200ml full-fat milk

pinch of Maldon or flaky salt

40g caster sugar

4 large egg yolks

300g dark chocolate (70 per cent cocoa
   solids), broken into pieces

100g white chocolate (20 per cent cocoa
   butter) in a block, frozen and grated or
   shaved (see *Quick Tip*), to finish

A good chocolate mousse recipe is a must in your pudding repertoire, and this one can be scaled up or down according to your needs. I guarantee that once you make this the first time, you'll go back and make it again and again. You can also make it in advance the day before you want to serve and keep it chilled in the fridge (add the white chocolate to finish, just before serving).

Soak the gelatine leaves in ice-cold water until softened, then squeeze out the excess water.

Meanwhile, make a crème anglaise by heating together 110ml of the cream, the milk, salt and half the caster sugar in a saucepan over a low heat until steaming.

In a medium bowl, whisk the egg yolks with the remaining sugar until combined. Pour the steaming milk onto the yolks and mix well. Return the mixture to the pan and stir over a medium heat until it has thickened – it should reach a coating consistency. Remove from the heat and pour into a heatproof bowl, stir in the soaked gelatine until it has dissolved, then set aside.

Meanwhile, melt the dark chocolate in a heatproof bowl, either in a microwave on low-medium power for 2–3 minutes in short (30-second) bursts, stirring after each burst, or over a bain-marie (place the bowl over a pan of gently simmering water, making sure the bottom of the bowl doesn't touch the water underneath), stirring occasionally.

Pour the crème anglaise into the melted chocolate and stir gently with a whisk until fully combined. Once this mixture has cooled enough to touch (you should be able to put your finger into it and not feel heat), but is still a pourable consistency, it is ready for the whipped cream.

Lightly whip the remaining 400ml of cream in a bowl until soft peaks form. Fold the whipped cream into the chocolate mixture until there are no lumps.

Pour the mixture into the serving dish or bowl, then cover and refrigerate for at least 4 hours or overnight to allow it to set before serving.

Scatter the grated/shaved white chocolate over the top of the chilled mousse just before serving, then serve with crème fraîche and a large spoon.

Leftovers will keep, covered, in the fridge for up to 2 days.

Quick Tip

Use a box grater, Microplane or vegetable peeler to grate or create shavings of white chocolate.

PASSION FRUIT TART

This tart is sharp and delicate, with a really beautiful texture. I find it's a perfect dessert to complement a spicy meal.

MAKES 1 X 20CM (8IN) TART; SERVES 8–10

Equipment

20cm (8in) round tart tin , fluted or straight-edged; sturdy flat baking tray

For the pastry

125g plain flour, plus extra for dusting

40g icing sugar

pinch of fine salt

80g cold unsalted butter, cubed

2 egg yolks

1 egg, beaten, for the egg wash

For the filling

200ml double cream

120g caster sugar

2 eggs

2 egg yolks

pinch of Maldon or flaky salt

juice of 4 passion fruits (see *Quick Tip* on page 159, but set the flesh and seeds aside for decorating the tart, if you wish)

juice of 2 large lemons

To make the pastry, in a stand mixer fitted with the paddle attachment, or a food processor, or in a large bowl, combine the flour, icing sugar and salt. Mix well. Add in the cold cubed butter and mix/pulse until the butter disappears and you have the texture of crumbs. If doing this by hand, rub into crumbs with your fingertips. Add the egg yolks and mix quickly to form a dough. Tip this out onto your workbench and gently knead to bring it together nicely. Flatten into a disc, wrap tightly in clingfilm and chill in the fridge for 2 hours or until firm. Or freeze it at this stage for up to 3 months (defrost before use).

Line the tart tin with the pastry by rolling it out on a lightly floured work surface to the thickness of 3–4mm (⅛in) or a £1 coin, leaving an overhang. Chill in the fridge for 30–60 minutes, or wrap and freeze for up to 3 months (defrost before use).

Preheat the oven to 160°C fan/180°C/gas mark 4. Place the sturdy baking tray on a shelf/rack in the centre of the oven to preheat.

Prick the base of the pastry case all over, line the tin with baking paper and fill to the top with baking beans or dry rice/lentils. Put this on the preheated baking tray in the oven and bake for 20–25 minutes or until the edges are lightly golden.

Carefully remove the baking paper and beans/rice/lentils from the tin. Return the pastry case to the oven (on the baking tray) for 15–20 minutes, until the base is golden. If it starts to rise up, simply prick the base with a fork.

Brush the tart all over with the beaten egg, then return to the oven for 3–5 minutes to form a seal. Remove from the oven and allow to cool slightly, then trim up the edges. Leave to cool completely before adding the filling. Reduce the oven temperature to 120°C fan/140°C/gas mark 1.

Make the filling. In a large pan, heat the cream and sugar together until the sugar is dissolved. In a heatproof mixing bowl, whisk together the eggs, egg yolks, salt, passion fruit juice and lemon juice. Pour the warm cream mixture over the egg mixture and whisk well to combine.

Pour this mixture into a blender and blend until smooth (or use a stick blender in the bowl). Pass the mixture through a fine sieve into a jug, then use a ladle to skim the surface to get rid of any air bubbles. Pour the mixture into the cooled blind-baked tart shell. Bake for 30–35 minutes or until it looks shiny and set, but there's a gentle wobble in the very middle.

Remove from the oven and allow to cool completely in the tin. Once cold, carefully remove the tart from the tin and place on a plate. Top with some of the leftover passion fruit flesh and seeds, if you wish. Serve in slices on its own or with pouring cream. This tart is best served on the day it's made, but leftovers will keep in an airtight container in the fridge for up to 2 days, then serve chilled.

Dinner

parties

I absolutely love hosting, and it's something I've enjoyed ever since my university days. I discovered my passion for cooking back then, and often found myself gathering random friends on the walk home, promising to feed them. These were usually just loose acquaintances that I only ever saw on nights out, often on the dance floor. But bringing people together over a table full of delicious food and drinks quickly became one of my favourite things to do.

Fast-forward to now, and you'll still find my dinner table full of guests, ready to enjoy a good meal and some great company. Of course, there's always an expectation when it comes to dessert in my house. As someone who always considers people's tastes, I make no less than three options – that way, everyone has a choice, or even better, they can try a little bit of each.

These dishes are designed to be easy to make ahead of time, so don't worry too much about presentation. Just make sure everything looks generous and inviting, and don't forget to stick a serving spoon in there. Above all, make sure you're enjoying yourself and relaxing – that's the most important part of any gathering.

CHOCOLATE AND CREAM PROFITEROLES

MAKES ABOUT 45 X 4CM (1½IN) CHOUX BUNS

This makes one of the most wonderful centrepieces to conclude a dinner party or to serve at a party. Make the recipe below or double it, as leftovers are good. I like eating chilled leftovers the next day when they're a bit too soft and the chocolate has set.

Equipment

3–4 flat baking trays

For the choux pastry

150ml water

150ml full-fat milk

150g unsalted butter

15g/1 tbsp caster sugar

5g/1 tsp fine salt

170g strong white flour

5–6 eggs, lightly beaten

25g demerara sugar

For the cream filling

600ml double cream

20g caster sugar

1 tsp vanilla bean paste

pinch of Maldon or flaky salt

For the chocolate sauce

250g dark chocolate (70 per cent cocoa solids), roughly chopped

180ml water

60g honey

pinch of Maldon or flaky salt

Make the choux. In a large saucepan, combine the water, milk, butter, caster sugar and salt. Bring this to a gentle simmer.

When it comes to a rolling boil, meaning the entire mixture is boiling rapidly as one, turn the heat down slightly and tip in the flour in one go. Use a sturdy wooden spoon or heatproof spoon and mix this vigorously until the mixture comes away from the sides of the pan.

Stir for a few minutes over a medium heat, then remove from the heat and tip into the bowl of a stand mixer or a large, heatproof bowl. Place a piece of clingfilm or baking paper on top so it is touching the mixture as it cools, to prevent it from drying out.

When this mixture has cooled to the touch, it won't take long (approx. 15 minutes), start adding the eggs, little by little, and mixing really well after each addition. Use the paddle attachment on a stand mixer to do this, an electric handheld whisk on a low setting (or you can use a food processor). You can also do this by hand but brace yourself because your shoulders will burn!

Once you've added about five of the eggs, test the mixture by picking it up with a large spoon out of the bowl, then give it a gentle nudge – you are looking for a 'dropping consistency'. This is when the mixture drops and flows ever so slightly easily without too much of a nudge. It shouldn't flow like a river, instead it should have a slight poise to it – you should be able to pipe it with ease, and it should hold its shape once piped.

If it's too wet, you'll need to start again, I'm afraid, but if you add the beaten eggs gradually, you should be able to avoid this completely. If the mixture is still quite firm and you think it will benefit from a little more egg, add the remaining beaten egg, little by little, until the mixture is at dropping consistency. Once you've reached this, it is ready to use.

Preheat the oven to 200°C fan/220°C/gas mark 7.

Take the baking trays and line each one with baking paper, securing the edges so they don't flap in the oven. If you don't have a lot of trays, that's ok, this batter will keep at room temperature if you need to rotate trays, just make sure you allow the trays to cool before piping onto them again.

Continued overleaf →

CHOCOLATE AND CREAM PROFITEROLES *continued*

Spoon the choux mixture into a piping bag fitted with a 1cm (½in) plain round nozzle. Pipe 4cm (1½in) rounds onto the lined baking trays, leaving a good 4cm (1½in) space between them, as they will grow and spread as they bake. Sprinkle the tops of the piped choux buns with the demerara sugar.

Bake for 15 minutes, but don't be tempted to open the door during this stage. Reduce the oven temperature to 180°C fan/200°C/gas mark 6, then bake for a further 10–12 minutes. The choux buns should easily come away from the paper, and they should be sitting proud and feel light and hollow.

Remove from the oven. Take a round piping nozzle and use the tip of the nozzle to create a hole in the base of each choux bun – this will be used as the point of entry to pipe the cream in later and doing this now helps to release excess steam. Transfer to a wire rack and cool completely.

Line a tray with baking paper. For the cream filling, gently whip the cream with the sugar, vanilla and salt until it reaches soft peaks and will hold its shape when piped into a choux bun.

Put the cream into a piping bag fitting with a round nozzle (approx. 1cm/½in). Fill each choux bun with cream by inserting the nozzle into the bottom of each one and pressing on the bag. Once each choux bun is filled, place it bottom-side down onto the lined tray. These will sit nicely in the fridge for up to 3–4 hours before stacking and serving with the sauce.

Make the chocolate sauce. Put the chocolate, water, honey and salt into a medium saucepan and heat gently. Stir frequently until the chocolate has melted and the mixture is silky, then keep stirring until it's glossy and smooth.

Remove from the heat, pour into a jug and allow to cool (at room temperature it will remain fluid).

To assemble the choux stack, loosely stack up the filled choux buns on a large serving plate/platter. Pour the chocolate sauce all over the stack, either at the table in front of your guests or in the privacy of your own kitchen. Serve and enjoy.

Once covered in chocolate sauce, the buns will keep in an airtight container in the fridge for up to 2 days. The texture changes and they soften quite a bit, but they remind me of supermarket profiteroles and éclairs, which isn't a bad thing to eat in front of the TV on a weeknight.

MANGO CRÈME BRÛLÉE

SERVES 5–6

Equipment

I use a 600ml ovenproof/casserole dish; roasting tray

400ml double cream

200ml mango purée (fresh or canned)

90g caster sugar, plus 4 tbsp for the brûlée

juice of ½ lime

100g egg yolks (approx. 5 yolks – see *Quick Tips*)

Quick Tips

Weigh the egg yolks if they look on the small side. Sometimes they can vary in size between 16–20g each.

The mango custard base can be made, baked, cooled and chilled up to 3 days in advance (keep it refrigerated). Brûlée it just before serving.

If you don't have a blowtorch, preheat the grill to high, then place the dish under the grill. Keep an eye on it as you will need to move it quite quickly as soon as the top starts to go golden, catch colour and bubble in a few places. Remove from the grill, then allow to cool before sprinkling the second layer of sugar on top, then repeat the grilling process. Remove from the grill and cool before popping it back into the fridge for 10 minutes before serving – when using a grill to caramelize a brûlée, often it can heat up the custard a touch too much, which is why it needs a bit of extra cooling time before you dig in.

If you want this for a large dinner party, double the recipe and bake it for longer, but just keep an eye out for the signs that it's done – indicated below. This is so good and refreshing in the summer months as it's low fuss and can be put together really quickly, and if your winter needs brightening up, make this.

Canned mango pulp/purée really is a good ingredient for providing hope and joy when it feels a bit glum outside. A good way of checking whether the quantity of mango mixture will fit into a dish that you want to use is to pop the dish on the scales, reset them to zero and weigh in 600ml of water – it should reach just below the top of the dish leaving an approx. 1cm (½in) gap. That's what you want.

Preheat the oven to 130°C fan/150°C/gas mark 2 and put the kettle on. You will need to bake this in a bain-marie, so first find a roasting tray that the ovenproof/casserole dish will fit comfortably in, as you will be filling the base of the roasting tray with hot water. Put the ovenproof dish inside its larger tray.

In a saucepan, heat together the cream, mango purée, 45g of the sugar and the lime juice over a low heat until steaming, stirring occasionally.

In a heatproof bowl, whisk the egg yolks with another 45g of the sugar until combined. When the cream mixture is steaming, pour it over the yolks and whisk to combine.

Pour this into the ovenproof dish, then transfer to the oven (in its roasting tray) being careful not to spill it. (You can also pour the egg mixture directly into the ovenproof dish once it's in the oven, if you prefer, but it depends on the angle of your oven door.) Once it's in, using a jug or the kettle, pour enough hot water into the roasting tray to reach halfway up the sides of the ovenproof dish containing the brûlée mixture.

Bake for 45 minutes. When it's ready, the custard should be set on top and the very middle should jiggle ever so slightly, but it shouldn't look wet. You should be able to lightly touch the edges with your fingertip and it should feel softly set.

Carefully remove from the oven and leave it in the hot water for a few minutes before you remove the dish from the bain-marie. Leave on the side to cool before transferring to the fridge to cool completely, as this is best served cold (see *Quick Tips*).

To brûlée, take the crème brûlée and if for any reason it looks wet on top, use a piece of kitchen paper to lightly touch the surface to remove this moisture. Sprinkle 2 tablespoons of the remaining sugar over the top (pick the dish up and tap the sides to distribute it evenly, if you need to). Wipe the edges clean as those will burn if the blowtorch touches them. Blowtorch the sugar until it's caramelized (see *Quick Tips*), then leave it to sit for 3–5 minutes until it's no longer hot. Repeat this process with the remaining 2 tablespoons of sugar and the blowtorch.

Allow to cool so the caramel sets hard and then serve immediately.

BROWN SUGAR MERINGUES WITH COFFEE CREAM AND CHERRIES

These meringues feel fantastically fancy, rich and decadent, but they are SUPER easy to make.

Equipment
2 large flat baking trays

For the meringues
150g egg whites (approx. 5 egg whites)

¼ tsp cream of tartar

230g soft dark brown sugar

2 tbsp cornflour

For the coffee cream
200g mascarpone cheese

60g caster sugar

pinch of Maldon or flaky salt

1 tbsp instant coffee granules, dissolved in 1–2 tbsp warm water

400ml double cream

To serve
200g tinned cherries in syrup or fresh cherries, pitted

50g grated chocolate (chocolate of your choice)

Preheat the oven to 100°C fan/120°C/gas mark ½. Line the baking trays with baking paper.

Make the meringues. In a clean bowl, either a large bowl or the bowl of a stand mixer, add the egg whites with the cream of tartar. Using an electric handheld whisk or the whisk attachment on the stand mixer, start whisking the whites on a medium speed until frothy and meringue-like. Add half of the brown sugar and whisk until thick, then add the remaining brown sugar and whisk on a medium speed until the meringue is really thick and stable. It should hold its shape – when you lift the whisk out of the meringue mix, it holds its shape in a stiff peak on the end of the whisk. If it's not there yet, keep whisking until it is. Add the cornflour and whisk slowly to combine, then stop whisking.

Using a large metal spoon, dollop the meringue onto the lined baking trays, leaving space in between each one as they will expand during baking. You'll make 6–8 large meringues.

Bake for 1½–2 hours. Test they are ready by gently lifting one off the paper – it should feel light and come away easily without sticking. If the meringue is resistant, it needs a little longer in the oven.

Remove from the oven and allow the meringues to cool completely on the trays before topping. The meringues will keep in an airtight container at room temperature for up to 3 days.

When you are ready to serve, make the coffee cream. In a large bowl, gently beat the mascarpone with a wooden spoon – basically, you want to smush it all around the sides of the bowl so that stirring in the cream is easy.

Add the sugar, salt and dissolved coffee granules and mix well. Add the cream and use a whisk to mix this together to form a stiff coffee cream.

To serve, spoon the coffee cream onto the meringues, then top with the cherries and finish with a generous grating of chocolate.

PEAR AND HAZELNUT DACQUOISE ROULADE

SERVES 6–8

Equipment

38 x 28cm (15 x 11in) Swiss roll-type tin or shallow (rimmed) baking tin/tray;

unsalted butter, for greasing

For the hazelnut dacquoise

180g egg whites (about 6 egg whites)

¼ tsp cream of tartar

80g caster sugar

pinch of fine salt

50g icing sugar, plus extra for dusting

65g roasted hazelnuts, coarsely chopped

50g ground almonds

For the poached pears

2 ripe pears

30g caster sugar

700ml water

juice of ½ lemon

1 cinnamon stick

For the cream filling

200ml double cream

1 tbsp honey

pinch of Maldon or flaky salt

This is a really good dessert for summer as it's light and refreshing. It also keeps really well for up to 3 days in the fridge. It just so happens to be gluten-free, too.

Preheat the oven to 150°C fan/170°C/gas mark 3½. Lightly grease and line the base and sides of the baking tin/tray with baking paper – this will help to release the baked sponge.

For the hazelnut dacquoise, place the egg whites and cream of tartar into a clean bowl, then whisk (either with an electric handheld whisk or in a stand mixer with the whisk attachment) until it is thick, firm and looks meringue-like. Add in the caster sugar and salt and whisk until stiff peaks form. Add in the icing sugar, 45g of the chopped hazelnuts and the ground almonds and fold in using a spatula. Spread the mixture evenly into the prepared baking tin/tray, then scatter the remaining hazelnuts over the top. Bake for 15–17 minutes until golden and dry to the touch.

Remove from the oven and allow the sponge to cool in the tin/tray for 5 minutes, then turn it out (invert) onto a wire rack, carefully peel off the lining paper and leave to cool completely.

Meanwhile, make the poached pears. Peel the pears, keeping them whole. In a medium saucepan, heat the sugar, water, lemon juice and cinnamon stick together over a medium heat, stirring until the sugar has dissolved, then bring to a simmer. Add the pears to the pan, place a piece of baking paper on top and place a small plate on top of the paper to hold the pears down in the liquid. Simmer gently for 25–30 minutes until the pears are soft when pierced with a knife.

Remove from the heat and allow the pears to cool completely in the syrup. Halve and core the pears, then slice them thinly or cut into cubes and set aside. Return the syrup left in the pan to a high heat and simmer rapidly until reduced by half, about 4–5 minutes. Remove from the heat, discard the cinnamon stick and set aside to serve with the dacquoise.

For the cream filling, whip the cream, honey and salt together in a bowl until soft peaks form. To assemble the dessert, slide the sponge onto a large sheet of baking paper keeping it the same way up (paper-lined side up, not baked-top side up). Spread the whipped cream evenly over the sponge, then evenly distribute the sliced or chopped pears on top. Carefully roll up the roulade from a shorter side (not a longer side), using the baking paper to help with this. Gently transfer the roulade to a large sheet of clingfilm, with the seam underneath, then wrap it tightly and twist both ends of the clingfilm to secure (this helps the roulade to keep its shape). Place on a tray, then refrigerate for 1 hour before serving.

To serve, carefully unwrap the roulade, place on a serving plate and dust with icing sugar, then cut into slices to serve.

This roulade keeps well in an airtight container in the fridge for up to 3 days.

CHOCOLATE AND SHERRY BAKED PEARS

MAKES 3 BAKED PEARS (6 HALVES), ENOUGH FOR 4–6 PEOPLE

These pears, although being very low effort and quick to assemble, are full of flavour and really moreish. Perfect served on their own or with ice cream. Don't let the marzipan throw you off, it bakes and starts to caramelize, giving the whole thing a lot more flavour.

Equipment
small roasting tray

3 large ripe pears
60g marzipan (natural/white or golden both work well)
30g dark chocolate (70 per cent cocoa solids)
2–3 amaretti biscuits
1 tbsp soft dark brown sugar
100ml dry sherry

Preheat the oven to 170°C fan/190°C/gas mark 5.

Peel the pears and cut them in half vertically. Using a teaspoon, remove the core and the middle of each pear half (you can enjoy the fleshy bits as a snack!), creating an indent big enough to house the filling, roughly the size of a tablespoon.

Chop the marzipan into small, bite-sized pieces, then chop the chocolate roughly to the same size. Crush the amaretti biscuits.

In a bowl, mix together the marzipan, chocolate, brown sugar and crushed amaretti biscuits. Pour in 20ml of the sherry and stir to coat.

Take a heaped tablespoon of the mixture and fill the indent in the middle of a pear with it, then repeat with all the remaining filling and pear halves.

Put the pear halves, stuffed-side up, in the roasting tray in a single layer, then pour over the remaining sherry and cover tightly with foil.

Bake for 30 minutes, then remove the foil and bake for a further 10 minutes until golden and sticky.

Remove from the oven and cool slightly, then serve the pears warm on their own or with ice cream or whipped cream.

These pears are best eaten freshly baked, but they can also be enjoyed cold or chilled.

They will keep in an airtight container in the fridge for up to 2 days. Reheat in a moderate oven for 7–10 minutes before serving.

TWO-TONE JELLY – RHUBARB JELLY AND VANILLA PANNA COTTA

The best people like jelly and this one is a thing of beauty, comprising two tones of contrasting colours and flavours, each complementing the other. The jelly can be made in individual dariole moulds, but it can also be set into serving glasses or made as one large jelly.

You'll need to make this dessert a couple of days or so before you want to serve it, to allow for setting time.

Continued overleaf →

'The best people like jelly and this one is a thing of beauty.'

MAKES 6 JELLIES OR 1 BIG JELLY FOR THE TABLE (SERVES 6)

Equipment

I used 6 dariole moulds, each with a capacity of 140–150ml, or use glasses of a similar capacity, or a large jelly mould (about 900ml capacity)

For the rhubarb jelly

400ml water

250g rhubarb, washed, trimmed and cut into 2cm (¾in) pieces

150g caster sugar

juice of ½ lemon

3 'platinum-grade' gelatine leaves (I use Dr. Oetker)

For the panna cotta

5 'platinum-grade' gelatine leaves (I use Dr. Oetker)

260ml full-fat milk

440ml double cream

140g caster sugar

pinch of Maldon or flaky salt

1 tsp vanilla bean paste

Make the rhubarb jelly. In a large pan, add the water, rhubarb, sugar and lemon juice. Bring to a simmer over a medium heat, then simmer, uncovered, for 10–12 minutes or until the rhubarb has softened to touch. Remove from the heat, transfer to a heatproof container and allow to cool, then cover and leave at room temperature for 2–3 hours, or overnight if you can, as this will deepen the colour.

Strain the rhubarb, reserving the liquid and discarding the rhubarb (or keep the rhubarb in the fridge and serve it over porridge or with granola and yogurt for breakfast).

Measure the rhubarb liquid – you will need 450ml of liquid for the three gelatine leaves. Soak the gelatine in ice-cold water until softened, then squeeze out the excess water. Meanwhile, pour 120ml of the rhubarb liquid into a small pan and heat gently until steaming. Add the soaked gelatine to the pan and whisk until dissolved, then pour this into the remaining rhubarb liquid and whisk well.

Put the dariole moulds (or glasses or larger mould) on a tray, then divide the rhubarb jelly mixture evenly between the moulds/glasses, filling them each halfway (or pour it all into the larger mould). Place in the fridge for at least 4 hours or overnight to set.

Make the panna cotta. Soak the gelatine in ice-cold water until softened, then squeeze out the excess water. Meanwhile, in a medium pan, heat the milk, cream, sugar, salt and vanilla together over a low-medium heat until steaming. Add the soaked gelatine to the pan and whisk well to dissolve the gelatine.

Pour into a shallow heatproof container, then leave this to cool at room temperature, whisking occasionally. It's important to do this as the vanilla will then disperse evenly through the mixture – if it's poured straight onto the rhubarb jelly, it will melt the jelly and the vanilla will sink.

Once the mixture is cooled completely, pour it over the set rhubarb jelly, dividing it evenly between each mould/glass (or pour it all into the larger mould). Return to the fridge for at least 4 hours or overnight to set.

To serve, dip each dariole mould briefly into hot water, then invert onto a serving plate, give it a gentle shake and remove the mould. Do the same for the larger mould (if using) and invert it onto a large serving plate, and just serve the desserts in the glasses, if using these.

Serve on their own or with some extra poached rhubarb and shortbread.

These desserts will keep (covered with clingfilm) in the fridge for up to 3 days.

SNAPPY CHOCOLATE AND CACAO NIB BISCUITS

MAKES ABOUT 18

Elegant and sophisticated, these biscuits make excellent gifts or a fancy biscuit tin top-up. They also pair perfectly with the Chocolate and Malt Baked Custard as pictured on page 137.

Equipment
large flat baking tray; 6.5cm (2¾in) round cookie cutter (optional)

85g plain flour
50g soft dark brown sugar
15g/1 tbsp cornflour
10g/2 tsp cocoa powder
10g/2 tsp cacao nibs
⅛ tsp Maldon or flaky salt
70g unsalted butter
20g honey
50g dark chocolate (70 per cent cocoa solids), broken into small pieces

Combine the flour, sugar, cornflour, cocoa powder, cacao nibs and salt in a bowl.

In a medium saucepan, combine the butter, honey and dark chocolate and cook over a low heat, stirring, until melted and smooth.

Remove the pan from the heat. Stir in the dry ingredients, using a wooden spoon or spatula to mix to form a loose, shiny dough.

Line a tray with baking paper. Spoon the dough onto the lined tray, cover it with clingfilm and refrigerate for at least 2 hours.

Remove the clingfilm, top the chilled dough with another sheet of baking paper and then roll out the dough on the work surface to roughly 3–4mm (⅛–¼in) thickness. Return to the fridge (on the tray) for 10 minutes.

Preheat the oven to 160°C fan/180°C/gas mark 4. Line the baking tray with baking paper and set aside.

Use the cookie cutter to cut the biscuit dough into about 18 rounds (or you can use a sharp knife to cut and portion the dough into rectangles instead). Transfer to the lined baking tray, leaving a small gap between each one.

Bake for 15–18 minutes or until they look dry.

Remove from the oven and allow to cool completely on the baking tray before eating.

These biscuits keep well in an airtight container at room temperature for up to 5 days.

CHOCOLATE AND MALT BAKED CUSTARD

SERVES 6

Equipment

600ml ovenproof/casserole dish
(see the intro for the Mango Crème
Brûlée recipe on page 125 for tips on
how to find the right dish); roasting tray

300ml double cream

100ml full-fat milk

2 tbsp malt powder

100g caster sugar

90–100g egg yolks (approx. 6 yolks)

pinch of Maldon or flaky salt

100g dark chocolate (70 per cent cocoa
solids), finely chopped, plus 20g extra
to finish

crème fraîche, to serve

If you're in need of a quick dessert for a dinner party, I would suggest you make this. It takes around 10 minutes to put together and the rest gets finished in the oven. It's really simple but incredibly elegant. Use really nice chocolate and serve with bowls of whipped cream and a plate of sweet biscuits (if you are in the mood to make everything from scratch, I'd suggest making the Snappy Chocolate and Cacao Nib Biscuits on page 135).

Preheat the oven to 130°C fan/150°C/gas mark 2 and put the kettle on. You will need to bake this in a bain-marie, so first find a roasting tray that the ovenproof/casserole dish will fit comfortably in, as you will be filling the base of the roasting tray with hot water. Put the ovenproof dish inside its larger tray.

In a medium saucepan, heat together the cream, milk, malt powder and half the sugar over a medium heat until steaming, about 5–8 minutes.

In a heatproof bowl, whisk the egg yolks, the remaining sugar and the salt together until combined. Set aside.

When the cream mixture is steaming, remove the pan from the heat, then whisk in the chopped chocolate until fully melted and combined.

Pour this over the egg yolk mixture and whisk well. I like to then use a stick blender to properly blitz this together – this is optional but it does help with the final texture.

Pour the mixture through a sieve into the ovenproof/casserole dish, then transfer to the oven (in its roasting tray) being careful not to spill it. Once it's in the oven, using a jug or the kettle, pour enough hot water into the roasting tray to reach halfway up the sides of the ovenproof dish containing the chocolate custard mixture.

Bake for 30 minutes or until lightly set but there's still a slight wobble in the middle.

Carefully remove from the oven and leave it in the hot water for a few minutes before you remove the dish from the bain-marie. Allow to cool fully at room temperature before placing in the fridge for 4 hours or until completely chilled.

Just before serving, grate the extra 20g of chocolate over the chilled pudding and then serve it with crème fraîche.

This pudding will keep, covered, in the fridge for up to 3 days.

MANGO AND SALTED MILK BAVAROIS

SERVES 5

Equipment

5 x 150ml dariole moulds
(or you can also set this in glasses)

2 'platinum-grade' gelatine leaves
   (I use Dr. Oetker)
350ml mango purée
   (canned or fresh – I use canned)
50ml full-fat milk
generous pinch of Maldon or flaky salt
finely grated zest and juice of 1 lime
400ml double cream
2 fresh ripe mangoes, peeled, stoned
   and sliced

Use the best fresh, ripe mangoes you can find to serve with this dessert and check seasonally which ones are available. For the bavarois, I use canned mango purée, as I'm a big fan of this and always have a can or two in my cupboard.

Soak the gelatine leaves in ice-cold water until softened, then squeeze out the excess water.

In a medium saucepan, gently warm the mango purée, milk and salt together until steaming. Remove from the heat and whisk in the soaked gelatine until it has dissolved. Whisk in the lime juice. Leave to cool at room temperature.

In a bowl, lightly whip 300ml of the cream until it forms soft peaks. Fold this through the cooled mango mix and use a whisk to get rid of any lumps.

Pour the mixture into the moulds (or glasses), dividing it evenly between them. Transfer to the fridge and leave to chill and set for at least 4 hours or overnight.

To serve, if you have used dariole moulds, briefly dip each mould in turn in hot water, wipe the water off and flip the bavarois onto a serving plate. Hold the dariole and the plate, give them a little shake, release the bavarois and remove the mould.

Serve each bavarois with some sliced mango, a spoonful of the remaining cream over the top (give it a quick whip first) and a sprinkling of lime zest.

MATTIE'S APPLE PIE

SERVES 8

Equipment
25cm (10in) round pie dish
or deep tart tin

For the pastry
420g plain flour, plus extra for dusting

210g cold unsalted butter, cubed, plus
    extra (softened) for greasing

120g golden caster sugar

1 tsp fine salt

5 egg yolks

For the apple filling
about 750g Bramley apples, peeled, cored
    and chopped into 3cm (1¼in) cubes
    (you need 600g prepared weight)

170g caster sugar

½ tsp Maldon or flaky salt

½ tsp vanilla bean paste

½ tsp almond extract

20g cornflour

To finish
1 egg, beaten, for the egg wash

demerara sugar, for sprinkling

icing sugar, for dusting

This is a slightly different fruit pie to the one you might expect. My Cherry Pie recipe on page 36 is based on an American-style fruit pie and the pastry there is salty and flaky. This pie, however, is more of a cross between a fruit tart and a pie. Mattie made it for me and I couldn't stop smiling.

For the pastry, place all the ingredients, apart from the egg yolks, in the bowl of a stand mixer fitted with the paddle attachment and mix on a low speed until you have breadcrumbs (or you can do this by hand by rubbing all the ingredients together using your fingertips to make breadcrumbs). Next, add in the egg yolks and mix until a dough is formed. Be careful not to overwork the dough.

Flatten the dough into a rough circle, then wrap in clingfilm and leave to rest in the fridge for a minimum of 1 hour or until firm.

While your dough is resting, add all the apple filling ingredients, apart from the cornflour, to a bowl and mix everything together, massaging the sugar into the fruit and allowing the flavours to get to know each other and macerate.

Preheat the oven to 180°C fan/200°C/gas mark 6. Grease the pie dish or tart tin with a little butter.

Once your pastry dough has rested, allow it to soften at room temperature for 10 minutes or so before rolling it out.

Cut off a third of the pastry dough and set this aside for the lid. Roll out the remaining two-thirds of the pastry on a lightly floured surface to about 30cm (12in) round and 4mm (¼in) thickness and use it to line the buttered dish or tin, pressing it in. Cut off any excess pastry from the top using a rolling pin or sharp knife.

Add the cornflour to the fruit mixture and make sure it's well incorporated, then spoon into the pastry case.

Roll out the reserved pastry for the lid (and any trimmings) to the same thickness. Egg wash the edges of the bottom pastry case and carefully place the pastry lid on top. Seal the edges by gently pressing the two together (and flute them, if you like). Pierce a small slit in the middle of the pie with a sharp knife to allow steam to escape. Brush the top of the pie with egg wash and then sprinkle with demerara sugar.

Bake for about 50 minutes or until golden brown.

Remove from the oven and allow the pie to rest for 20 minutes before serving. Add a dusting of icing sugar just before serving. Serve warm with cold cream or custard.

Leftovers can be kept in an airtight container in the fridge for up to 3 days, then eaten cold or warmed through in a hot oven.

TIERED CELEBRATION PAVLOVA

I used to be responsible for making the tiered pavlovas for the weddings at St. JOHN in London during my time as a pastry chef there. What I loved the most was that we would make them all year round, with the fruit changing each season, meaning you'd get to play with poaching and roasting fruits like quince, pears, plums and rhubarb, or using the best fresh seasonal berries you could buy, such as cherries, strawberries, blackberries, etc. The meringues would be made in varying sizes so you could stack them on top of each other, sandwiched together with cream and fruit.

This celebration dessert is made for sharing with a crowd of family and friends (it serves about 50!) and is definitely something that needs to be assembled à la minute. Get a jug of fruit coulis/sauce ready for the person celebrating so that they can pour it all over the top just before serving.

'This celebration dessert is made for sharing with a crowd.'

MAKES 1 LARGE TIERED PAVLOVA; SERVES ABOUT 50

Equipment
3 flat baking trays

For the meringue
480g egg whites (approx. 16 egg whites)
20ml white wine vinegar
1 tbsp vanilla bean paste (optional)
800g caster sugar
120g cornflour

For the cream filling
1 litre double cream
100g caster sugar
2 tbsp vanilla bean paste
large pinch of Maldon or flaky salt

To assemble and serve
1kg fresh seasonal berries of your choice, rinsed and dried, sliced if needed
300ml fruit coulis of your choice (see *Quick Tips*)

I would suggest breaking the meringue quantity down and making it in three parts so that it fits into a stand mixer, making all of the meringue mixture before dividing it between the three lined baking trays. One baking tray will then have a large round meringue layer approx. 25–30cm (10–12in) in diameter, another baking tray will have a 20cm (8in) round meringue layer, and the final baking tray will have a 10–15cm (4–6in) round meringue layer. The larger meringue round will use more of the total meringue mix than the other two, with the smallest meringue round using the least.

Preheat the oven to 100°C fan/120°C/gas mark ½. Line the three baking trays with baking paper.

For each quantity of meringue (using a third of the ingredients for each batch, rounding the vinegar and sugar up or down slightly to divide fairly evenly), place the egg whites, white wine vinegar and vanilla (if using) in the clean bowl of a stand mixer with the whisk attachment. Whisk on a medium speed for 7–10 minutes, past the frothy stage, until you see soft peaks form (you can also make this in a large mixing bowl with an electric handheld whisk, if you prefer).

Keeping the mixer on, start adding the sugar to the egg whites, a tablespoon at a time. Gradually increase the speed of the mixer as you do so. By the time you add the last of the sugar, you should be whisking on a medium-high speed (by not whisking on a high speed to start with, you avoid large air bubbles in your mix, which can cause an uneven texture when baking). Continue whisking for 2–3 minutes until stiff peaks form and the meringue is thick and glossy. At this point, add in the cornflour, mixing slowly at first and gradually increasing the speed until it is all mixed in. Stop here, as you don't want the meringue to deflate. Gently scrape the meringue into a large 'holding' bowl and set aside. Wash and dry the stand mixer bowl and whisk attachment.

Continued overleaf →

TIERED CELEBRATION PAVLOVA

continued

Repeat to make the other two quantities of meringue mixture in the same way.

Spread the meringue (as detailed at the start of the method) into one large flat round on one lined baking tray, into a medium flat round on another lined baking tray, and into a smaller flat round on the third lined baking tray. Place them all in the oven at the same time, each on a different oven shelf.

Bake the larger round for about 3 hours, the medium round for about 2 hours and the smallest round for about 1½ hours or until dry (but not coloured). You will know when each one is done as it should easily lift off the paper.

Remove the meringues from the oven and leave to cool completely on the baking trays, before carefully peeling off the paper (see *Quick Tips*).

Make the cream filling. In a large bowl, lightly whip the cream with the sugar, vanilla and salt until it forms soft peaks.

To assemble the pavlova, place the largest meringue layer on a serving platter. Spread with some of the cream filling, then top with some of the fruit. Place the medium-sized meringue layer on top, spread with more cream filling and top with more fruit. Place the smallest meringue layer on top, then top this with the remaining cream filling and fruit.

Serve immediately, cut into slices, with the fruit coulis served in a jug for pouring over.

The pavlova is best eaten freshly made and assembled. If you do have leftovers, they will keep in an airtight container in the fridge for up to 2 days, but the meringue layers will soften.

Quick Tips

To make a simple raspberry coulis, using a blender or food processor, blend together 300g of fresh raspberries, 70g of icing sugar and the juice of ½ lemon, then strain through a fine sieve, discarding the seeds. Taste the coulis and add a little more icing sugar, if needed. Pour it into a jug to serve. Alternatively, you can simply serve ready-made shop-bought coulis from a jar instead.

Once baked and cooled, the meringue layers will keep, tightly wrapped in cling-film, in a dry place at room temperature or in an empty cold oven, for up to 2 days.

JEWISH CHEESECAKE

MAKES 1 X 20CM (8IN) CHEESECAKE; SERVES 8–10

Equipment

20cm (8in) springform cake tin;
larger shallow casserole dish or
roasting tray

120g digestive biscuits, crushed

60g unsalted butter, melted, plus extra
(softened) for greasing

280g cream cheese

150g caster sugar

100ml double cream

150g sour cream

1 tbsp plain flour

large pinch of Maldon or flaky salt

finely grated zest of 1 lemon

3 eggs, separated

20g rum-soaked raisins (see *Quick Tip*
on page 187) (optional)

I couldn't write another baking book without including a recipe for a cheesecake, but it had to be one I hadn't yet tried. Although I've eaten quite a bit of Jewish cheesecake from various delis, I hadn't tried to make one myself. So I asked Mattie to call up his Poppa for this one and then tested the finished result on his dad.

Lightly grease and line the bottom and sides of the springform cake tin with baking paper.

Make the base. In a bowl, mix together the crushed biscuits and melted butter until completely combined. Press the biscuit mixture over the bottom of the lined tin to create a base, using the back of a metal spoon to do this, pushing the crumb mixture just a touch up the sides of the tin as well. Chill in the fridge while you prepare the filling.

Preheat the oven to 160°C fan/180°C/gas mark 2. Fill the kettle and put it on to boil.

Take a large piece of foil and wrap it securely around the bottom of the springform tin (to cover the join where the bottom and sides of the tin meet and clip together) – this is because the cheesecake is baked in a bain-marie and you don't want water to get into the cheesecake.

Make the filling. In a large bowl, beat the cream cheese with 100g of the sugar, the sour cream, double cream, salt and lemon zest, then mix through the egg yolks, followed by the rum-soaked raisins (if using).

In a separate bowl, either in a stand mixer with the whisk attachment or in a large bowl using an electric handheld whisk, whisk the egg whites until thick and meringue-like, then add the remaining sugar and whisk until glossy and thick. Carefully fold the meringue into the cream cheese mixture, being careful not to overmix. Pour this into the tin over the biscuit base.

Carefully place the springform tin into the larger shallow casserole dish or roasting tray, then transfer to the oven, being careful not to spill it. Once it's in, using a jug or the kettle, pour enough hot water into the casserole dish/roasting tray to reach halfway up the sides of the dish/tray containing the cheesecake.

Bake for about 45–60 minutes or until the cheesecake is golden around the edges with a very slight wobble in the middle.

Remove from the oven, then remove from the bain-marie. Leave the cheesecake to cool completely in the tin, then chill in the fridge for 4 hours before serving.

To serve, carefully remove the cheesecake from the tin, transfer it to a plate and serve in slices. Serve on its own or with some fresh berries in the summer.

This cheesecake will keep in an airtight container in the fridge for up to 3 days.

MINT CHOCOLATE CHIP SEMIFREDDO

SERVES 6–8

Equipment
freezerproof bowl/container

170ml double cream

30g fresh mint leaves

green food colouring gel

pinch of Maldon or flaky salt

180g caster sugar

50ml water

90g egg whites (approx. 3 egg whites)

50g dark chocolate (70 per cent cocoa solids), melted

Make this delicious semifreddo for the table as one of your after-dinner desserts. It will sit nicely alongside a few fruity desserts and is perfect for those who like after-dinner chocolate mints. It's also a great dessert to make ahead as it keeps in the freezer for up to 1 month.

In a high-powered blender, blend the cream and mint together until the mint is finely chopped throughout. Pass this through a fine sieve into a large bowl and discard what's left in the sieve.

Whip the mint cream to soft peaks with the food colouring and salt – I use a cocktail stick or toothpick to add the food colouring gel as I go until I reach a mint green colour. Set aside.

Next, make the Italian meringue. Place the sugar and water in a medium saucepan and cook over a medium heat until boiling, then continue to boil rapidly and test the temperature using a sugar thermometer.

Meanwhile, whisk the egg whites in a stand mixer until frothy. When the sugar syrup reaches 110°C/230°F, turn the mixer speed up so the egg whites start to look like meringue. When the sugar syrup reaches 119°C/246°F, remove it from the heat and pour it gently down the side of the bowl while whisking, then whisk on a medium speed until the meringue mixture has cooled down.

Add the meringue to the whipped cream and fold together until combined.

Pour a third of the meringue/cream mixture into the freezerproof bowl/container and drizzle in a third of the melted chocolate, gently folding it in as you go so that it is rippled/marbled throughout. Repeat with another third of each of the meringue/cream mixture and melted chocolate. Fold in the final third of the meringue/cream mixture, then drizzle the remaining melted chocolate on top. Cover with clingfilm or a lid and place in the freezer overnight.

Serve the semifreddo straight from the freezer in scoops.

The semifreddo will keep in the freezer for up to 1 month.

MASCARPONE AND SLICED PEACHES

SERVES 6

Equipment
large bowl; 6 tea plates

200g mascarpone cheese
50g icing sugar
pinch of Maldon or flaky salt
4 medium-ripe fresh peaches in season

I ate this in Bologna when the weather was just starting to turn cold but it was still warm enough to sit outside for lunch in a coat. This was one of my most memorable meals at Drogheria della Rosa, recommended by chef Hugo Harrison. After enjoying the most divine pastas to start, we finished the meal with a dish which translated to 'mascarpone and peaches'. I thought to myself, how good can that be? It was a lesson in simplicity and good ingredients – sliced fresh peaches with a little bite sat on top of cold beaten mascarpone, an excellent way to finish a meal.

The trick with this is to beat the mascarpone down until it loses its body and turns to liquid, then to serve it cold, and to use really nice, juicy peaches.

In a large bowl, beat the mascarpone until it is smooth, then mix in the icing sugar and salt until combined. Use a large wooden spoon to continuously beat the mascarpone until it becomes a runny texture.

Divide the mascarpone between six small plates (I use small tea plates that I've chilled in the fridge).

Halve, stone, then thinly slice the peaches and divide them between the plates. Serve immediately.

RHUBARB AND CUSTARD PIE

Make this as soon as you can get your hands on the first forced rhubarb of the year. It will make you (and your guests!) smile.

This recipe and the other two pies that follow all utilize a biscuit base, and the three pies served together and spaced out along a dinner table are a must-try trio for when you have lots of guests who like to eat!

'It will make you (and your guests!) smile.'

SERVES 12–14

Equipment
25cm (10in) round pie dish (I use my shallow Le Creuset dish for this pie); large baking tin

For the biscuit base
200g sweet oaty biscuits (such as Hobnobs)

50g crunchy/snappy ginger biscuits (such as Ginger Nuts)

100g unsalted butter, melted

For the custard filling
600ml full-fat milk

300ml double cream

150g caster sugar

1 tsp vanilla bean paste or 1 vanilla pod, split in half lengthways and seeds scraped out

pinch of Maldon or flaky salt

2 eggs

2 egg yolks

50g cornflour

For the rhubarb topping
700g forced rhubarb, trimmed and chopped into 5–7.5cm (2–3in) pieces

150g caster sugar

30ml water

2 dried hibiscus flowers (optional)

15g/1 tbsp crushed pistachios, to finish

For the biscuit base, crush both lots of biscuits into breadcrumbs, either by putting them in a food bag and bashing with a rolling pin or blitzing in a food processor. Tip the biscuit crumbs into a bowl and stir through the melted butter. Tip the crumb mix into the pie dish and lightly press with the back of a metal spoon to form an even layer over the bottom of the dish. Refrigerate while you make the custard filling and the rhubarb topping.

Meanwhile, make the custard filling. In a large saucepan, heat the milk, 200ml of the cream and 75g of the sugar with the vanilla and salt over a low heat until steaming, stirring occasionally.

In a heatproof bowl, whisk the eggs and yolks together. Stir the cornflour and the remaining 75g of sugar together, then slowly whisk this into the egg mixture until combined.

Pour three-quarters of the steaming milk onto the egg mixture and whisk to combine, then pour this back into the pan, whisking. Increase the heat to medium and heat, whisking constantly, until bubbling. Continue whisking for 3–4 minutes until the custard has thickened. Remove from the heat, whisk in the remaining cream, then pour into a heatproof container and cover the surface with clingfilm (this prevents a skin forming on the top). Allow to cool, then chill the custard in the fridge for 2–3 hours – it will set and become slightly gelatinous.

In the meantime, prepare the rhubarb topping. In a large bowl, mix the rhubarb and sugar together, then set aside for 30 minutes.

Preheat the oven to 160°C fan/180°C/gas mark 4.

Arrange the rhubarb in a single layer in the baking tin. Spoon over the water and add the hibiscus flowers (if using). Roast for 15 minutes or until slightly tender but still holding its shape. Remove from the oven and allow to cool, then leave at room temperature until you are ready to use it. Remove the hibiscus flowers (if using).

To assemble the pie, gently beat the custard to make it spoonable, then spread it evenly over the biscuit base. Refrigerate for a minimum of 1 hour.

To finish, using a slotted spoon, top the custard with the roasted rhubarb (keep the roasting syrup to drizzle on top), then scatter with the crushed pistachios and drizzle over some rhubarb roasting syrup. Serve in slices.

Leftovers will keep in an airtight container in the fridge for up to 3 days.

LEMON MERINGUE PIE

SERVES 12–14

This is my version of a speedy lemon meringue pie. I am completely omitting the lemon curd and instead opting for a lemon posset filling.

Equipment
25cm (10in) round pie dish (I use my shallow Le Creuset dish for this pie)

For the biscuit base
250g digestive biscuits

100g unsalted butter, melted

For the lemon posset filling
600ml double cream

150g caster sugar

finely grated zest of 2 lemons

juice of 4 lemons (approx. 120ml)

For the Italian meringue
250g caster sugar

50ml water

150g egg whites (approx. 5 egg whites)

For the biscuit base, crush the biscuits into breadcrumbs, either by putting them in a food bag and bashing with a rolling pin or blitzing in a food processor. Tip the biscuit crumbs into a bowl and stir through the melted butter. Tip the crumb mix into the pie dish and lightly press with the back of a metal spoon to form an even layer over the bottom of the dish. Refrigerate while you make the lemon filling.

For the lemon posset filling, in a large pan (make sure it's large as this mixture is boiled so you don't want it boiling over onto the hob), gently heat the cream and sugar together, stirring, until the sugar has dissolved. Bring to the boil over a medium heat, then add in the lemon zest and lemon juice. Whisk well and bring back to the boil, then continue to boil for 2–3 minutes, whisking constantly until very slightly thickened. Remove from the heat, pour into a heatproof bowl and allow the mixture to cool. Once cool, pour the lemon posset mixture over the biscuit base in the pie dish. Leave to set in the fridge for 4 hours or overnight.

Make the Italian meringue. Place the sugar and water in a medium saucepan and cook over a medium heat until boiling, then continue to boil rapidly and test the temperature using a sugar thermometer.

Meanwhile, whisk the egg whites in a stand mixer until frothy. When the sugar syrup reaches 110°C/230°F, turn the mixer speed up so the egg whites start to look like meringue. When the sugar syrup reaches 119°C/246°F, remove it from the heat and pour it gently down the side of the bowl while whisking, then whisk on a medium speed until the meringue mixture has cooled down.

Spoon the meringue on top of the lemon mixture, covering it completely and peaking the top attractively. Blowtorch the meringue until nicely browned, then serve immediately. If you don't have a blowtorch, place the pudding under a preheated hot grill to brown the meringue, but keep an eye on it, making sure it doesn't catch.

This pie is best eaten on the day it is made.

BANOFFEE PIE

SERVES 12–14

Equipment

25cm (10in) round pie dish (I use my shallow Le Creuset dish for this pie); rimmed baking tray

For the biscuit base

250g digestive biscuits

100g unsalted butter, melted

5g/1 tsp cacao nibs

2 bananas (approx. 120g each with skin on), peeled and sliced

For the caramel layer

1 x 397g can ready-made caramel

pinch of Maldon or flaky salt

220ml double cream, lightly whipped to soft peaks

For the cream topping

400ml double cream

pinch of Maldon or flaky salt

1 tbsp caster sugar

For the caramelized bananas

50g caster sugar

2 tbsp dark rum

4 bananas (approx. 120g each with skin on), peeled and sliced diagonally

20g dark chocolate (70 per cent cocoa solids), to finish

The caramelized rum bananas on top of this decadent and popular pie are optional, and instead you can serve regular sliced bananas with shaved chocolate on top, but if you have time, definitely give them a go.

For the biscuit base, crush the biscuits into breadcrumbs, either by putting them in a food bag and bashing with a rolling pin or blitzing in a food processor. Tip the biscuit crumbs into a bowl and stir through the melted butter. Tip the crumb mix into the pie dish and lightly press with the back of a metal spoon to form an even layer over the bottom of the dish, bringing the crumb mix a touch up the sides, too.

Sprinkle over the cacao nibs and then layer over the sliced bananas. Set aside.

Make the caramel layer. Tip the caramel into a bowl and gently beat until smooth, then sprinkle in the salt and fold in the whipped cream. Pour this evenly over the bananas in the dish, then chill in the fridge for 1 hour.

Make the cream topping. In a bowl, lightly whip the cream with the salt and sugar until soft peaks form. Spread this over the top of the chilled pie in an even layer. Return to the fridge while you make the caramelized bananas.

For the caramelized bananas, line the baking tray with baking paper. Put the sugar into a large frying pan and cook over a medium heat until melted, then continue to cook for about 2–3 minutes, swirling the pan occasionally, until the sugar has caramelized to a deep amber colour. Carefully pour in the rum and let it sizzle, then add in the banana slices and gently toss in the caramel to coat.

Remove from the heat, then spoon the bananas onto the lined baking tray, spreading them out a bit. Leave to cool.

To finish, top the pie with the caramelized bananas, then grate the chocolate over. Serve immediately in slices.

Leftovers will keep in an airtight container in the fridge for up to 3 days.

PASSION FRUIT GRANITA WITH WHITE CHOCOLATE CREAM

SERVES 4

Equipment

shallow freezerproof container;
4 iced thick (freezerproof) glasses
(see *Quick Tips*)

For the passion fruit granita

75g caster sugar

75ml water

juice of 5 large passion fruits, seeds
discarded (see *Quick Tips*)

juice of 2 limes

150ml smooth orange juice

pinch of fine salt

5ml/1 tsp vodka (optional)

For the white chocolate cream

200ml double cream

100g white chocolate (20 per cent cocoa
butter), chopped

½ tsp vanilla bean paste (optional)

Quick Tips

To ice your serving glasses, an hour
before serving, I place the serving
glasses into the top drawer/section
of the freezer.

To extract the juice from passion fruits,
I like to gently roll each passion fruit on
my workbench before I cut them in half
for juicing. I then scoop out the inner
flesh/pulp over a fine sieve and use the
back of a spoon to press the flesh/pulp
and juice through (discard the seeds left
in the sieve).

Serve this refreshing passion fruit granita piled high in iced glasses with the white chocolate cream alongside at the table. A delicious dessert!

Make the granita. In a small saucepan, heat together the sugar and water until the sugar has dissolved. Remove from the heat and allow to cool.

Blend the passion fruit juice, lime juice, orange juice, sugar syrup and salt together in a blender or food processor until thoroughly combined, adding the vodka (if using). Pour into the shallow freezerproof container, cover and freeze for 2 hours.

Remove from the freezer and agitate/stir the mixture with a fork, then return to the freezer for a further 1 hour. Repeat the stirring/scraping with the fork and freeze for another hour. Repeat the stirring/scraping and freeze for another 30 minutes, then repeat the stirring/scraping again.

Cover and return the mixture to the freezer and leave to freeze completely, checking it every so often – when it's ready, it should have a crystal-like texture. If it starts to freeze more like a block, use a fork to scrape it back to the texture of granita.

Meanwhile, make the white chocolate cream. In a medium saucepan, heat the cream over a medium-low heat until steaming, then add the white chocolate and vanilla (if using) and stir over a low heat until the chocolate has melted fully. Remove from the heat and leave to cool before serving at room temperature.

To serve, using a fork, scrape the granita into iced glasses (see *Quick Tips*). Pour the white chocolate cream into a nice jug and serve with the granita.

Once it's ready, the granita will keep in the freezer for up to a week.

QUEEN OF PUDDINGS

SERVES 6

Equipment

15cm (6in) round cake tin or casserole/ovenproof dish

For the pudding base

250ml full-fat milk

50g unsalted butter, plus extra (softened) for greasing

finely grated zest of 1 lemon

100g fresh breadcrumbs (white are best but sourdough breadcrumbs or brown breadcrumbs will also work)

50g caster sugar

2 egg yolks

For the raspberry compote

140g fresh raspberries

a few lemon verbena leaves (when in season – omit if not in season), shredded

For the Italian meringue

100g caster sugar

20ml water

2 egg whites

I thought I wasn't much of a fan of this pudding after making it reluctantly at St. JOHN and I couldn't quite understand the appeal. However, Doug McMaster of Silo in Hackney, London, worked on a version with me for his zero waste cooking school, utilizing my Italian meringue technique and his take on lowering some of the sweetness. Doug omitted the sweet layer (typically, jam would be used) and instead cut through the sweetness with tart sharp raspberries and fresh shards of lemon verbena. We used leftover sourdough breadcrumbs when we made this together.

It's best eaten as soon as it's made, preferably when raspberries are in season!

Preheat the oven to 150°C fan/170°C/gas mark 3½. Lightly grease and line the base of the cake tin with baking paper (this will help to remove it from the tin). Alternatively, make the pudding in a lightly greased casserole/ovenproof dish and serve it straight from the dish.

For the pudding base, heat the milk in a small pan over a low heat until it is simmering. Remove from the heat, stir in the butter and lemon zest, then stir through the breadcrumbs.

In a bowl, whisk the sugar and egg yolks together until combined. Pour the milk mixture onto the egg yolk mix and stir together, then leave to sit for 20 minutes – the breadcrumbs will swell in this time. Pour into the prepared cake tin or casserole dish.

Bake for 20 minutes or until golden all over and dry to the touch.

Remove from the oven and allow to cool in the tin/dish, then remove from the tin (if using) and place the baked base on a serving plate (or just leave the baked base in the casserole dish, if using).

Make the compote. Gently warm the raspberries in a saucepan until they break down, about 5 minutes. Spoon the raspberry compote over the baked base, then top with the lemon verbena leaves (if using). Set aside.

Make the Italian meringue. Place the sugar and water in a medium saucepan and cook over a medium heat until boiling, then continue to boil rapidly and test the temperature using a sugar thermometer.

Meanwhile, whisk the egg whites in a stand mixer until frothy. When the sugar syrup reaches 110°C/230°F, turn the mixer speed up so the egg whites start to look like meringue. When the sugar syrup reaches 119°C/246°F, remove it from the heat and pour it gently down the side of the bowl while whisking, then whisk on a medium speed until the meringue mixture has cooled down.

Top the pudding base generously with the meringue mixture, covering it completely and lifting the meringue into peaks as you go, then blowtorch to lightly brown it and serve immediately. If you don't have a blowtorch, place the pudding under a preheated hot grill to brown the meringue, but keep an eye on it, making sure it doesn't catch.

This pudding is best eaten as soon as it's made.

Weekend

bakes

If you have some free time on a lazy weekend, this is where you should start. These bakes are perfect for when you have the luxury of time and can take things at your own pace. It could be something you've been wanting to master, like bread or a more complex recipe. When you have time and space, like a whole weekend, it can feel a lot easier to accomplish things that might ordinarily be difficult.

As with so many things, practise helps you improve each time. For example, the pastéis de nata took me many, many attempts to nail down and get right. No matter how many times I thought I knew what I was doing, I learned something new each time – my touch and feel improved, and soon enough, I really got the knack for assembling and baking them. I want to reassure you that even if it does take time, it's incredibly satisfying when you finally get there.

DUTCH BABY PANCAKES WITH BLUEBERRY COMPOTE

MAKES 4 SMALL PANCAKES OR 1 LARGE PANCAKE (SERVES 4)

Equipment

4 x 15cm (6in) cast iron skillets, or
1 x 25cm (10in) cast iron skillet/heavy-based frying pan

For the blueberry compote

200g frozen blueberries

30g caster sugar

splash of water

For the Dutch pancakes

120g plain flour

1 tbsp caster sugar

pinch of fine salt

3 large eggs

120ml full-fat milk

½ vanilla pod, split lengthways and seeds scraped out, or ½ tsp vanilla bean paste

4 tbsp neutral oil, such as sunflower, vegetable or rapeseed oil, for cooking

icing sugar, for dusting

These are so quick and fun to make and eat. The magic of a Dutch baby pancake is the way it puffs up in the oven, but you've got to be fast and ready to eat them as soon as they're cooked, as they deflate once they start to cool. These make an impressive start to your day served with fruit compote or even enjoyed as dessert after dinner with ice cream.

The batter is very similar to a Yorkshire pudding batter, but you need to make sure that you give it enough time to sit before cooking, as this will help the gluten in the flour to absorb the liquid.

Ideally, use individual cast iron skillets to cook these in as the skillets retain heat really well. Otherwise, a heavy-based frying pan will also work as long as it's ovenproof. Preheating the skillets/pan in the oven first will give the batter a kick start as soon as it's poured in.

Be careful when cooking these, as everything gets quite hot!

Make the blueberry compote. In a saucepan, stir together the blueberries, sugar and a splash of water. Cook over a medium-low heat for 10 minutes until the blueberries have started to break down. Remove the pan from the heat and leave the compote to cool before using.

Make the Dutch pancake batter. In a large bowl, stir together the flour, sugar and salt. Crack the eggs into the middle of the bowl. Start whisking the eggs, gradually bringing in the flour from the edge of the bowl. Gradually add the milk to the bowl, whisking well to form a smooth batter. Finally, whisk in the vanilla seeds or paste. Cover the bowl with a tea towel and set aside at room temperature for 1 hour.

Preheat the oven to 180°C fan/200°C/gas mark 6.

Place the individual skillets or large skillet into the oven for 5 minutes to get hot. Remove from the oven and pour 1 tablespoon of oil into each skillet or all of the oil into the large skillet. Divide and pour the batter into the individual skillets or pour it all into the large one and quickly put the skillet(s) back into the oven. Bake the individual skillets for 10–12 minutes or the large one for 18–20 minutes until the pancakes are puffy and golden all over.

Remove from the oven and serve quickly straight from the pans as these pancakes deflate quickly (serve the large pancake from the pan, too, with a knife to portion).

Dust the pancakes with icing sugar and serve with the blueberry compote and some Greek yogurt for breakfast, or serve them with the blueberry compote and some ice cream, crème fraîche, whipped cream or sweetened mascarpone for dessert. Eat immediately!

BREAD PUDDING

SERVES 12

Equipment

28 x 18 x 5cm (11 x 7 x 2in) baking tin

unsalted butter, for greasing

750g raisin bread, crusts removed and cut into 2cm (¾in) cubes (see *Quick Tip*)

200ml full-fat milk

100ml water

350g soft dark brown sugar

3 eggs

40ml rum

1 tbsp mixed spice

pinch of Maldon or flaky salt

30g mixed peel

2 large cooking apples (500g total weight – Bramleys work really well), peeled, cored and grated

100g shredded vegetable suet

2 tbsp demerara sugar

2 tbsp icing sugar (optional)

Not to be confused with bread and butter pudding, this is really stodgy and I don't mean that in a bad way – stodgy in a sustenance type of way. If you have family members who grew up in the UK, make them a tray of this, as it's pure nostalgia and actually very very good.

Preheat the oven to 150°C fan/170°C/gas mark 3½. Lightly grease and line the base and sides of the baking tin with baking paper.

Put the bread cubes into a really large bowl. Pour the milk and water over, then use your hands to really squelch it all together so that the bread starts to absorb the liquid and soften.

In a separate bowl, mix together the soft brown sugar, eggs, rum, mixed spice, salt, mixed peel and grated apple.

Sprinkle the suet over the mushed bread mix and then add in the egg/sugar mixture. Use your hands to mix it all together really well – this is the fun bit.

Tip the bread mixture into the prepared tin and spread out, making sure it's evenly pressed into the tin, then sprinkle over the demerara sugar.

Bake for 30–40 minutes or until it's dry to the touch, has formed a slight crust and feels firm to the touch.

Remove from the oven and allow to cool in the tin before dusting with the icing sugar (if using) and portioning to serve. This can be served warm with custard and/or toffee sauce or cold as it is.

Leftovers will keep in an airtight container in the fridge for up to 3 days, or will freeze for up to 1 month (defrost before eating).

Quick Tip

You can use frozen bread for this, just defrost it before using. If you don't want to use raisin bread, use up odds and ends of other bread and add in 30g of raisins. The bread should be a sourdough style raisin bread or regular white bread without raisins which can then be added. If you use a brioche style or fruit loaf the recipe will be too dense and rich.

JAPANESE MILK LOAF

Equipment

20 x 10 x 10cm (8 x 4 x 4in) loaf tin;
heavy flat baking tray (optional)

175ml water
335g strong white flour
40g unsalted butter, softened
80ml full-fat milk
7g/1½ tsp Maldon or flaky salt
40g caster sugar
7g (1 sachet) easy-blend dried yeast
1 egg
neutral oil, for greasing

To make this Japanese milk loaf, I'm using a technique called tangzhong. This technique originated in Japan and was subsequently shouted about by Taiwanese chef Yvonne Chen. It yields a much softer textured bread that rises really well and stays fluffy for a lot longer. It involves pre-cooking a portion of the flour from the recipe in water or milk before adding it (cooled) to the dough. What happens here is that the flour absorbs the liquid really well, creating a stable structure for the starch in the flour to hold onto that liquid. So once it's baked, the result is a lovely fluffy-textured loaf.

This is a really fun way to make soft pillowy bread, and one that lasts for longer and can be turned into the most delicious French Toast.

For the tangzhong, combine the water and 35g of the flour in a medium saucepan. Stir this continuously over a low-medium heat for a few minutes until it starts to form a thick paste. Transfer the mixture to the bowl of a stand mixer.

Add the butter on top while the mixture is still warm, then add the milk. Mix together using the dough hook for a few minutes or until it has come together and is evenly mixed. The mixture should now have cooled down. If not, set aside until it has cooled.

In a separate bowl, add the remaining flour, the salt and sugar and stir together really well. Add the yeast and stir. Add this to the mixer bowl, along with the egg. Mix on a medium speed using the dough hook for 10–15 minutes, occasionally scraping down the sides of the bowl. By this stage, it should be elastic, shiny and dough-like.

Oil a large bowl well. Transfer the dough to the oiled bowl and leave it, covered with a damp tea towel, in a warm place for 30 minutes.

Use your hands to fold the dough into itself on each side until you've done this four times. Cover and leave it to rest for another 30 minutes, then repeat the folding.

Lightly grease and line the base and sides of the loaf tin with baking paper.

Tip the dough into the tin using a dough scraper. As this dough is quite wet and very forgiving, it's not being shaped here as you would often do for a loaf. Cover as before and leave the dough to prove in a warm place for 2–3 hours or until it has grown in size and almost doubled and it feels really light to touch. It should look supple and feel soft – check by lightly pressing your finger into it, it should spring back gently and not remain indented.

Continued overleaf →

JAPANESE MILK LOAF *continued*

Preheat the oven to 170°C fan/190°C/gas mark 5.

Cover the tin with an ovenproof lid if it comes with one or put the heavy baking tray on top of the tin – this is going to help achieve a nice compact loaf that bakes evenly.

Bake for 20 minutes, then reduce the oven temperature to 160°C fan/180°C/gas mark 4 and bake for another 20 minutes. Remove the lid/tray and bake for another 10 minutes or until golden and shiny – it should feel light and look well risen. Tap the underside once removed from the oven, it should sound hollow.

Remove from the oven and allow to cool completely in the tin, then turn out and slice to serve.

This bread is fantastic eaten fresh on the day it is made, but it also keeps really well wrapped tightly or in an airtight container at room temperature for 3–4 days. It works well toasted if there is any left after that.

'This is a really fun way to make soft pillowy bread.'

HOT CROSS BUNS

MAKES 12

Equipment
large flat baking tray

For the tangzhong and dough
180ml full-fat milk

400g strong white flour, plus extra for dusting

7g/1½ tsp Maldon or flaky salt

50g caster sugar

7g (1 sachet) easy-blend dried yeast

2 eggs

50g unsalted butter, softened

20g mixed peel (optional)

finely grated zest of 1 lemon

2 tsp ground cinnamon

1 tsp ground allspice

neutral oil, for oiling bowl

For the raisin mix
150g raisins

5g/1 tsp tea leaves or 2 tea bags of your choice (I like Rooibos)

approx. 250ml boiling water, to cover

1 cinnamon stick

For the crosses
60g plain flour

15g/1 tbsp icing sugar

60ml full-fat milk

2 tbsp apricot jam, to glaze

Here, I use the Milk Loaf recipe method (see page 170) to achieve soft, fluffy hot cross buns that keep for days without drying out. The method is a touch different because of the fruit that is added in – the fruit gets soaked in tea before being strained and kneaded through the dough. You can also switch the quantity of soaked fruit for an alternative like chocolate chips, if you prefer.

You can start these the day before baking, if you like, as the dough can be proved in the fridge overnight (this is preferable).

Make the tangzhong. Combine the milk and 40g of the flour in a medium saucepan. Stir this continuously over a low-medium heat for a few minutes until it starts to form a thick paste. Use a hand-held whisk to avoid any lumps.

Once the mixture has thickened, remove from the heat and transfer to a heatproof container. Place a piece of baking paper directly on top of the mixture and allow to cool fully at room temperature before refrigerating until cold. You can do this a day ahead or a few hours before.

Make the raisin mix. Place the raisins in a heatproof bowl. Brew some tea, using the tea of your choice, with enough boiling water to be able to cover the raisins. Strain the brewed hot tea over the raisins, add the cinnamon stick and leave this to sit for 1 hour, then strain before use (discarding the soaking liquid and cinnamon stick).

Make the dough. In the bowl of a stand mixer, mix together the remaining flour, the salt and sugar and combine well. Add the yeast and stir. Add the cold tangzhong mixture and the eggs before mixing with a dough hook until combined. Continue to mix on a medium–high speed for 10–15 minutes, occasionally scraping down the sides of the bowl as needed. By this stage, it should be elastic and dough-like. Add the softened butter and mix for a further 10 minutes until the butter is incorporated and the dough is shiny and elastic. Cover the bowl loosely with a clean tea towel and leave to relax for 20 minutes.

Add the strained raisins, the mixed peel (if using), lemon zest and ground spices to the dough. Mix well for 10 minutes on a medium speed until the dough is smooth and elastic. Scrape down the sides of the bowl as needed. The dough should hold together as one, if not, mix for longer and increase the speed to bring it together.

Continued overleaf →

HOT CROSS BUNS *continued*

Oil a large bowl well. Transfer the dough to the oiled bowl and leave to prove at room temperature for 2 hours or until doubled in size.

Line the baking tray with baking paper and lightly dust your hands and work surface with flour. Portion the dough into 12 (each dough ball will weigh about 70g). Shape each portion into a ball and place on the prepared baking tray, lining them up so they are next to each other, 3 x 4 – they shouldn't be tightly touching but it's ok if they are close together. Cover with the tea towel and leave to prove in a warm place for 30–60 minutes or until they are soft, springy and puffy.

Preheat the oven to 170°C fan/190°C/gas mark 5.

For the crosses, combine the flour, icing sugar and milk in a small bowl to make a smooth paste. Transfer to a piping bag fitted with a small plain nozzle. Pipe a cross onto the top of each bun.

Bake for 15 minutes, then turn the tray and bake for another 15 minutes, until the buns are evenly golden and shiny on top.

Remove from the oven and cool slightly before brushing the buns with the beaten apricot jam to glaze (if the apricot jam is still quite thick, microwave it briefly until it loosens up). Transfer the buns to a wire rack to cool completely.

Serve split and toasted or untoasted, on their own or with some butter.

These buns keep well in an airtight container at room temperature for up to 4 days.

CARDAMOM BUNS

MAKES 12

Equipment

large flat baking tray

For the dough

5 green cardamom pods

100g unsalted butter

500g strong white flour, plus extra for dusting

75g caster sugar

½ tsp Maldon or flaky salt

7g (1 sachet) easy-blend dried yeast

2 eggs

180ml full-fat milk, plus 2 tbsp for the egg wash

vegetable oil, for greasing

For the cardamom butter

10 green cardamom pods

200g unsalted butter, at room temperature

150g soft light brown sugar

pinch of Maldon or flaky salt

For the sugar syrup

100g caster sugar

150ml water

pared long strips of zest from 1 lemon

juice of ½ lemon

These can be made fairly quickly if you wake up in the morning in the mood for something like a cinnamon bun in the afternoon – we've all been there, haven't we? I've also added a recipe for Saffron Buns using the same dough. You could split the dough in two and make half of the cardamon filling and half of the saffron filling to get the best of both worlds.

Make the dough. Crush the cardamom pods and remove the seeds, then use a pestle and mortar to crush them into a powder. Melt the butter in a small pan, then add the crushed cardamom and gently heat so that it's just slightly warm to touch, it shouldn't be scalding or steaming. Remove from the heat.

In the bowl of a stand mixer, mix the flour, caster sugar and salt together really well. Add the yeast on one side of the bowl, then one egg on the other side along with the 180ml of milk and the melted warm cardamom butter. Using the dough hook, mix slowly until a rough dough forms. Turn the speed up to medium and mix for 10–15 minutes or until a smooth, shiny, elastic dough forms.

Oil a large bowl, then transfer the dough to this bowl and cover with a damp tea towel. Leave at room temperature for 1½ hours or until it has risen up and is light and puffy.

Meanwhile, make the cardamom butter. Crush the cardamom pods, remove the seeds and crush them in a pestle and mortar to make a powder. Beat the butter in a bowl with the brown sugar, salt and crushed cardamom seeds until combined (you can do this in a food processor, if you prefer). Set aside at room temperature until you are ready to use it.

Line the baking tray with baking paper.

Pat the risen dough down to remove the air (knock it back) and then tip it out onto a very lightly floured workbench. Roll out the dough to 50 x 60cm (20 x 24in).

Spread the cardamom butter evenly over the dough, right up to the edges. Fold the dough in half widthways making it 25 x 60cm (10 x 24in), then cut this length into 12 even strips, each about 5cm (2in) wide.

To make each bun, take one of the strips and cut it down the middle, leaving a join at the top, then twist both strips together. Roll up from the joint end into a spiral bun shape, tucking the loose ends under the bun, then place on the prepared baking tray. Repeat with all the remaining strips to make 12 buns in total, leaving space between each bun on the tray as they will grow in size as they bake.

Cover the tray with a damp tea towel or a lightly greased piece of clingfilm and leave to prove at room temperature for about 20 minutes or until they are soft and have expanded slightly (if you touch them with your fingertip, the dough should spring back).

Meanwhile, make the syrup. Heat the sugar and water together in a small pan until the sugar has dissolved. Add the strips of lemon zest and the lemon juice, then cook over a medium heat for 4–5 minutes until bubbling. Remove from the heat and allow to cool slightly – you want the syrup to be warm but not hot. Carefully remove the strips of lemon zest before using.

Preheat the oven to 170°C fan/190°C/gas mark 5.

Beat together the remaining egg and the 2 tablespoons of milk in a small bowl to make an egg wash. Brush the risen buns with the egg wash.

Bake for 18–22 minutes or until golden in places and expanded. Turn the tray and bake for a further 4 minutes or until golden all over.

Remove from the oven and allow the buns to cool on the baking tray for 15 minutes before spooning over the warm syrup. Serve warm.

These are best eaten on the day they are made.

SAFFRON BUNS

To make these, follow the recipe on page 176 for Cardamom Buns but use the saffron butter and saffron syrup (see opposite) instead of the cardamom butter and sugar syrup, and sprinkle over some nibbed/pearl sugar just before baking.

MAKES 12

Equipment
large flat baking tray

30–40g nibbed sugar or pearl sugar

For the saffron butter
1 tbsp full-fat milk

generous pinch of saffron strands

180g unsalted butter, at room
    temperature

150g soft light brown sugar

pinch of Maldon or flaky salt

For the saffron syrup
100g caster sugar

150ml water

pinch of saffron strands

juice of ½ lemon

pinch of Maldon or flaky salt

Make the buns as on page 176 using the saffron butter (see method below) instead of the cardamom butter. Just before baking, brush the risen buns with the egg wash, then sprinkle over the nibbed/pearl sugar and bake as above.

For the saffron butter, gently warm the milk in the microwave for a few seconds, then add the saffron strands and leave it to sit for 10 minutes. Beat the butter in a bowl (or in a food processor) with the brown sugar, salt and saffron milk mixture until combined. Use as instructed above.

For the saffron syrup, heat the sugar and water together in a small pan until the sugar has dissolved. Add the saffron strands, lemon juice and salt and cook over a medium heat for 4–5 minutes, as on page 177.

Remove the buns from the oven and allow them to cool on the baking tray for 15 minutes before spooning over the warm saffron syrup. Serve warm.

These are best eaten on the day they are made.

CRÊPES WITH ROASTED RHUBARB AND ORANGE CREAM

MAKES 6

Equipment

large rimmed baking tray; large frying pan (approx. 26cm/10½in diameter)

1 x quantity of crêpes (see page 213), cooked

200g rhubarb, stalks trimmed and cut into 2cm (¾in) pieces

75g caster sugar

½ vanilla pod, split in half lengthways and seeds scraped out, or ½ tsp vanilla bean paste (optional)

finely grated zest and juice of 2 oranges

300ml double cream

pinch of Maldon or flaky salt

2 tbsp icing sugar, plus extra for dusting

6 tsp unsalted butter

20g crushed roasted pistachios (optional)

I used to serve crêpes seasonally on the menu at Llewelyn's in London, so this is my type of dessert. It has excellent mouthfeel – light, crisp, buttery, fruity, creamy, all of that!

Make the crêpes according to the instructions on page 213, then stack them on a plate and set aside.

Meanwhile, for the roasted rhubarb, toss the rhubarb pieces with the caster sugar, vanilla (if using) and the zest and juice of 1 orange in a bowl, then let it sit for 1 hour.

Preheat the oven to 160°C fan/180°C/gas mark 4.

Take the rimmed baking tray, tip the macerated rhubarb onto it and spread out in a single layer. Bake for 10–12 minutes or until the rhubarb is tender but not falling apart. Remove from the oven and allow to cool on the baking tray before using, and keep the juice as you will use it to spoon over the crêpes.

Make the orange cream. In a bowl, whip the cream, salt, icing sugar and the remaining orange zest and juice together until it forms soft peaks or readily stands up on a spoon. Set aside.

Reheat the cooked crêpes, one at a time. Melt 1 teaspoon of the butter in the large frying pan over a low heat. Add a crêpe to the pan and gently fry in the butter for 1–2 minutes to heat it up and coat lightly, then flip it over and repeat. Transfer to a serving plate and serve immediately or keep warm in a low oven while you reheat the rest. Repeat with the remaining butter and crêpes, stacking the warm crêpes on top of each other, if you like, separating them with a sheet of baking paper between each one.

Serve each crêpe, folded into quarters, with some roasted rhubarb (and juices) spooned over, a dollop of orange cream, a scattering of pistachios (if using) and a dusting of icing sugar. Serve immediately.

RUM AND RAISIN PUDDING

Equipment

15 x 20cm (6 x 8in) rectangular pie tin/ ovenproof dish; sturdy flat baking tray

60g unsalted butter, softened, plus extra for greasing

60g caster sugar

2 eggs, beaten

80g plain flour

1 tsp baking powder

pinch of Maldon or flaky salt

50g rum-soaked raisins (see *Quick Tip*)

60ml full-fat milk

60ml double cream

1 tbsp custard powder

1 tbsp golden syrup

I am a big raisin fan, and, despite not ever drinking, one of my favourite ice cream flavours (since I was a child) is rum and raisin. There is something so delicious about rum raisins. You might have noticed my love of rum raisins through my previous recipe writing, so if you're like me, I advise always keeping a Kilner jar of them in the cupboard (see *Quick Tip* below).

Preheat the oven to 170°C fan/190°C/gas mark 5. Lightly grease the pie tin/ ovenproof dish.

Beat the butter and sugar together in a large bowl until pale and fluffy. Stir in the eggs and mix well – it will look like it has split a bit but don't worry, it's ok.

In a separate bowl, stir together the flour, baking powder and salt, then add to the creamed mixture and fold together. Stir in the rum-soaked raisins. Scoop the batter into the pie tin/ovenproof dish and spread evenly.

In a jug, stir together the milk, cream, custard powder and golden syrup until combined. Pour this mixture over the raisin batter and use a butter knife to swirl it through the batter.

Put the pie tin/ovenproof dish on the sturdy baking tray and bake for 40 minutes or until it looks cakey and golden all over.

Remove from the oven and serve warm with custard or chilled cream and extra rum-soaked raisins, if you like.

Quick Tip

To make the rum-soaked raisins, place 50g of raisins in a bowl, add 20ml of rum and stir together. Leave to soak for 1 hour. This will give you around 50g of rum-soaked raisins for the recipe, but double or treble the quantity if you would like extra to serve. It's also best to do this ahead of time in a large batch, as they will keep for months on end in a sealed container (like a Kilner jar) at room temperature out of direct sunlight.

PASTÉIS DE NATA

MAKES 20

Equipment
20 individual pastéis de nata tins/moulds, or 2 x 12-cup muffin tins; rimmed heavy baking tray

For the puff pastry
300g strong white flour, plus extra for dusting

1 tsp fine salt

60g cold unsalted butter, cubed

100ml water

240g unsalted butter, chilled but malleable (not rock hard)

For the custard filling
525ml double cream

105g caster sugar

1 cinnamon stick

1 pared strip of lemon rind

70g Glucose

175g egg yolks (approx. 9 yolks)

pinch of Maldon or flaky salt

These Portuguese custards tarts are a proper labour of love and one that you should keep working on if you want to perfect them! With pastéis de nata, it's all about getting the knack and working with your schedule and oven to ensure you get the desired finish – crunchy, crisp, light pastry filled with a sweet, scented, silky custard, so moreish that you'll want to eat a few, one after the other.

It took me a while to come up with a recipe that works for domestic ovens, one that ensures a crisp pastry and a smooth custard that doesn't split or unevenly colour. I ended up, after many iterations, finding that a cream-based custard works really well, although non-traditional. Typically, the filling would feature milk, a sugar syrup and egg yolks. However, after countless trials I found the cream-based custard more robust and reliable for this sized batch.

Make the puff pastry. In a large bowl, or the bowl of a stand mixer fitted with the paddle attachment, or in a food processor, mix together the flour and salt. Add the 60g of cold cubed butter and rub in using your fingers, or mix well/pulse until the butter has disappeared. Mix in the water until a rough dough forms, then bring it together with your hands. Tip the dough out onto a sheet of baking paper, then flatten into a rectangle roughly the size of an A4 sheet of paper. Place on a tray, cover with clingfilm or baking paper, then chill in the fridge for 2 hours or until firm.

Prepare the remaining 240g of butter by shaping it into a smaller rectangle than the dough one in the fridge – to roughly the size of an A5 sheet of paper.

Take the dough out of the fridge and dust your work surface with flour. With a short side nearest to you, gently roll out the dough vertically until it's only slightly longer than a sheet of A4 paper.

Put the butter on the dough so it fits roughly over two-thirds of the bottom of the dough. Fold the top third of the dough down over part of the butter and then fold the bottom third (with the rest of the butter on it) up over the first fold. Turn the dough 90 degrees to the right. This is called a single turn.

Roll the dough vertically to the same size as before, then repeat the above by folding the top third down and the bottom third up and over the first third, then turn by 90 degrees. Cover and rest in the fridge for 2 hours.

Continued overleaf →

PASTÉIS DE NATA *continued*

Take the dough out of the fridge. Roll the dough out vertically as before, but this time complete a double turn by folding the top quarter down to the centre and the bottom quarter up to the centre before folding these two pieces together to close it like you would a book, then turn it 90 degrees, cover and rest in the fridge for 2 hours. Repeat the double turn and then cover and rest in the fridge for another 2 hours. The pastry is now ready to use – keep it chilled (overnight is fine) until you are ready to use it.

Roll out the pastry on a lightly floured surface to a rectangle about 5mm (¼in) thick. It will measure approx. 38 x 40cm (15 x 16in). Trim the edges to neaten them up – this should take you to approx. 32 x 35cm (12½ x 14in). Starting from the long side, roll it up tightly into a spiral log. Wrap it in clingfilm or baking paper and chill in the fridge for 2 hours (it keeps refrigerated for up to 3 days and it also freezes well for up to 1 month; defrost overnight in the fridge before use).

To achieve really nice spirals of pastry I would recommend slicing off a couple of centimetres from each end (see *Quick Tip*). Cut the pastry log across (widthways) into 20 equal pieces, each approx. 1.5cm (⅝in) wide. Line each pastéis de nata tin/mould (or muffin cup) by placing a piece of pastry into the bottom of the tin/mould (or muffin cup). Use your fingers to press the pastry flat into the bottom, then up the sides, working it with your thumbs to evenly press the pastry around the inside of the tin/mould (or muffin cup). Create a small edge above the tin/mould (or muffin cup) as it will shrink down slightly during baking. Place these prepared lined tins/moulds on the baking tray (for ease of transferring them) and chill in the fridge for 30 minutes.

Make the filling. In a medium saucepan, heat the cream with the sugar, glucose, cinnamon stick and lemon rind until the sugar has dissolved, then bring to just below a simmer. Remove from the heat and allow to cool briefly, then discard the cinnamon stick and lemon rind.

In a large bowl, whisk the egg yolks to break them up with the salt. Pour over the warm cream mixture and whisk well until fully combined. Leave the mixture to cool to room temperature, then strain the custard through a sieve set over a jug (for ease of pouring).

In the meantime, preheat the oven to 250°C/gas mark 10, or your highest oven setting (I find that these bake better in a hot oven rather than with the fan setting). While the oven is preheating, put a flat, heavy baking tray in the oven to heat up.

When you're ready to bake the tarts, carefully remove the hot tray from the oven and put it on a flat, heatproof surface. Place the prepared pastry cases on the tray (this helps to crisp the bottom of the pastry) and pour the custard into the pastry cases, filling each one three-quarters full. Bake the tarts (on the baking tray) in the oven for 10–12 minutes or until the top is bubbling, the custard is browned and the pastry is golden and flaky.

Remove the tarts from the oven and cool in the tins/moulds (or muffin cups) for 5 minutes, then carefully remove and transfer them to a wire rack. Serve warm. These tarts are best eaten warm on the day they are made, but leftovers will keep in an airtight container in the fridge for up to 2 days to be enjoyed chilled.

Quick Tips

I like to use pastéis de nata tins/moulds but you can also use greased muffin tins, (though the baked result will be slightly different).

The pastry can be started the day before to help with time. It can also be frozen for up to 1 month, once it's been rolled into a spiral log and tightly wrapped in clingfilm.

If you are short of time, you can use ready-made chilled (or frozen, defrosted) puff pastry instead. Use about 700g of ready-made puff pastry (in a block, or ready-rolled), then follow the instructions from step 7 onwards).

Any scraps and offcuts of pastry can be gathered together and used to make mini palmiers or frozen to gather enough for a pie lid.

PALMIERS

MAKES 16

Equipment
flat baking tray; 2 large rimmed baking trays

1 x quantity of puff pastry (see page 189)
plain flour, for dusting
80g caster sugar

Palmiers are incredibly underrated for how special they are. It works nicely to keep a batch of puff pastry in the freezer, ready to whip up a quick batch of these for rainy days, or for when you need a crunchy accompaniment for a baked dessert like the Chocolate and Malt Baked Custard (see page 136) or the Mango and Salted Milk Bavarois (see page 139) featured in the book.

Line the flat baking tray with baking paper and set aside.

Follow the instructions on pages 189–190 for making the puff pastry. Once the pastry has been chilled for the final time, cut the pastry in half, then roll out each portion of pastry on a lightly floured surface to a rectangle about 5mm (¼in). It will measure approx. 38 x 40cm (15 x 15¾in). Sprinkle the sheets of pastry evenly all over with 40g (in total) of the caster sugar.

Working with one sheet at a time, starting from one of the long edges, roll each sheet of pastry up tightly to the centre, then repeat from the other side so the two rolls meet in the centre to make a palm leaf shape or butterfly shape. Transfer both 'scrolls' to the lined baking tray, then chill in the fridge for 20 minutes.

Preheat the oven to 200°C fan/220°C/gas mark 7 and line the two rimmed baking trays with baking paper.

Place two small pieces of baking paper on the workbench to help roll the palmiers, and put the remaining 40g of caster sugar into a small bowl (which you'll use to dip each palmier in before rolling).

Working with one 'scroll' at a time, cut each chilled pastry roll across into 2.5–3cm (1–1¼in) slices. Take each slice (one at a time) and dip it into the sugar on both flat (cut) sides, then place each one onto one piece of baking paper, place the other piece of baking paper on top and use a rolling pin to roll it out, lengthways, to approx. 2mm (¹⁄₁₆in) thickness. Transfer each palmier to one of the lined baking trays, leaving space between each one. Repeat for each palmier to make 20 in total (see *Quick Tips*).

Continued overleaf →

PALMIERS *continued*

Bake for 18 minutes before flipping over and returning to the oven for a further 4 minutes or until deep golden, caramelized and flaky.

Remove from the oven and allow to cool completely on the baking trays before serving.

These palmiers are best enjoyed on the day they are baked, even while still a touch warm, with a cuppa.

Leftovers will keep in an airtight container at room temperature for up to 2 days, but make sure you separate them with baking paper between to stop them sticking to each other.

Quick Tips

Palmiers should be baked within the same hour that the sugar is added – this is because the sugar starts to weep and liquify and will affect the baked result if left any longer before baking.

If you are short of time, you can use ready-made chilled (or frozen, defrosted) puff pastry instead. Use about 700g of ready-made puff pastry (in a block, or ready-rolled).

BAKED NECTARINES

SERVES 4

Equipment
shallow baking or casserole dish

4 medium-ripe nectarines in season
50g golden caster sugar
splash of Marsala (optional)
6–8 amaretti biscuits, crushed
4 scoops of vanilla ice cream

I have very fond memories of eating these when I was a teenager. My aunt made them once after dinner, then my mum and I kept trying to recreate them. A few months later, we found a recipe in a local magazine and kept it by the fridge. Every now and then, we'd decide to make baked nectarines after dinner, serving them with vanilla ice cream from our local ice cream parlour. They called it vanilla but I distinctly remember it containing no vanilla, instead it was whiter than white and tasted more like milk.

Preheat the oven to 160°C fan/180°C/gas mark 4.

Halve the nectarines, leaving the stones in place in four of the halves. Place the nectarine halves, cut-side up, in the baking/casserole dish, making sure there's enough space for them to sit in a single layer.

Sprinkle the sugar evenly over them and then the Marsala (if using). Use your fingers to toss the nectarines in the sugar, then turn them so they are skin-side up.

Bake for 15–18 minutes or until the skins are starting to blister slightly and the sugar is bubbling.

Remove from the oven, then leave the nectarines to sit for 5 minutes before serving. Remove the stones before serving (they should slip out easily), then sprinkle the nectarines with the crushed amaretti biscuits and serve each portion with a scoop of ice cream.

These baked nectarines are best served warm from the oven.

FLOURLESS CHOCOLATE FONDANT WITH A CARAMEL CENTRE

One of the very first pastry jobs I had involved making hundreds upon hundreds of chocolate fondants, daily. Despite there being other really good desserts on the menu, the chocolate fondant was a signature and it wasn't going anywhere.

At first, I wasn't so sure about this fondant as it took a lot of work, so much preparation and a minimum of two people to assemble them as the batter would harden quite quickly. We'd then have to make a well in the centre of each one, by hand, to allow for some piped caramel to fill the centre. The last job involved covering the caramel with a fresh batch of fondant to stop the caramel leaking out during baking.

During my time there and during service, we'd inevitably have one or two that would leak. I would be grateful for these as I could use them as bargaining chips to get me after-service fried rice, sushi, tempura or something savoury from one of the other chefs.

I wanted to include a nice fondant recipe here, but one that felt a bit easier, so I use mini caramel-filled chocolate eggs to get that nice centre.

The unbaked fondants need to be refrigerated for at least 4 hours (or overnight) before baking, so they are ideal for making in advance the day before you want to bake and serve them.

Continued overleaf →

'The chocolate fondant was a signature.'

FLOURLESS CHOCOLATE FONDANT WITH A CARAMEL CENTRE *continued*

MAKES 4 FONDANTS

Equipment
I used 4 dariole moulds, each with a capacity of 140–150ml

80g unsalted butter, plus extra (softened) for greasing the moulds

100g dark chocolate (70 per cent cocoa solids), chopped

2 eggs

2 egg yolks

45g caster sugar

10g/2 tsp cocoa powder, sifted, plus extra for dusting the moulds and serving

pinch of Maldon or flaky salt

4 mini caramel-filled chocolate eggs (I used Galaxy Chocolate Caramel Mini Eggs, but you can use any mini caramel-filled chocolate eggs or mini chocolate eggs that have a runny filling, without a hard sugar coating, i.e. mini creme eggs or mini praline eggs would work well, too)

Butter the dariole moulds really well and dust with cocoa powder, then place in the fridge.

Melt the butter and chocolate together in a heatproof bowl, either over a bain-marie or in short bursts in a microwave until fully melted.

In the bowl of a stand mixer with the whisk attachment, or in a large bowl using an electric handheld whisk, whisk the eggs, egg yolks and sugar together until slightly thickened.

Pour in the melted butter and chocolate mixture and mix well with a wooden spoon or a spatula. Finally, fold in the measured sifted cocoa powder and the salt until a homogeneous mixture forms.

Spoon the mixture into the prepared dariole moulds, dividing it evenly and leaving a 2cm (¾in) space at the top of each. Take your mini caramel-filled chocolate eggs and push one into the centre of each fondant. Use a spoon to guide the fondant mixture over each caramel egg so it's covered.

Refrigerate for 4 hours or overnight (you can also freeze them at this point for up to 1 month, then bake from frozen as below, adding on an extra 3–4 minutes baking time).

When you are ready to bake, preheat the oven to 180°C fan/200°C/gas mark 6.

Bake the fondants for 10–12 minutes or until they have risen slightly to the top of the moulds and no longer look wet in the middle.

Take the fondants out of the oven and leave to stand for 1 minute before turning each one out onto a serving plate and carefully removing the mould. Dust with sifted cocoa powder. Serve immediately with ice cream.

These are best eaten straight away.

Savoury

bakes

You'll be pleased to know that I have finally convinced my mum to share her samosa recipe for this book. It's not that she's possessive in any way – she just thinks some things are common sense and cannot be written down. However, I managed to persuade her otherwise and her recipe is included in this chapter.

I've also included methi (fenugreek) parathas, which were a significant part of my childhood and a subject of debate as to who makes them better – my mum or Biji?

I love this chapter so much that I've thoroughly enjoyed testing and writing it. The chicken pie is a massive hit among my friends and has graced my dinner table many times. With savoury dishes, you can freestyle a bit more, switch up the flavours, and adjust the seasoning to suit you, so make sure to taste as you go.

CRUMPET PANCAKES

Equipment

15cm (6in) small frying pan (with a lid,
    if required – see method)

450ml full-fat milk

1 tbsp caster sugar

7g (1 sachet) easy-blend dried yeast

270g strong white flour

25g plain wholemeal flour

1 tsp bicarbonate of soda

¼ tsp fine salt

neutral oil, for cooking

**These are extremely low fuss, giving you the crumpet texture without the need
for crumpet rings. They cook faster and work well as a vessel for breakfast
toppings, both sweet or savoury, and they are very moreish.**

Warm the milk in a pan over a low heat so it's just warm to the touch (tepid) not hot.
Remove from the heat.

In a medium heatproof bowl, stir together the sugar and yeast. Add the warm milk
and stir well. Cover with a damp tea towel and leave to sit at room temperature for
20–30 minutes until it has almost doubled in volume and there are lots of air pockets
on top.

In a large bowl, mix both flours together with the bicarbonate of soda and salt. Pour in
the yeasty milk mixture and whisk together to form a batter. Cover and set aside at room
temperature for a further 30 minutes. Give it a quick stir before use.

To cook the crumpet pancakes, add a drizzle of oil to the small frying pan and warm
over a medium heat. Ladle in enough (an eighth) of the batter to cover the base of the
pan. Cook until bubbles appear on top, about 4 minutes. Now either place a lid on top
and allow the crumpet pancake to steam, or if you prefer, flip it over and cook for a few
minutes on the other side before serving. Remove to a serving plate and keep warm in a
low oven, while you repeat with the remaining batter (adding a little extra oil to the pan
each time) until they are all cooked. You will make eight in total.

Serve the crumpet pancakes warm for breakfast with butter and jam or with cream
cheese, smoked salmon and cucumber, or whatever takes your fancy.

The cooled cooked crumpet pancakes will keep in an airtight container in the fridge for
up to 3 days. Warm through before eating, either in a toaster or with a little oil in a small
frying pan over a medium heat for a minute or two on each side.

CARAMELIZED ONION TATIN

SERVES 4 AS A STARTER

Equipment

15cm (6in) non-stick, ovenproof
frying pan

4–6 Roscoff pink onions or red onions,
    cut in half (or enough onion halves to
    cover the base of the pan)

2 tbsp caster sugar

2–3 sprigs of thyme

large pinch of Maldon or flaky salt

1 tbsp sherry vinegar

plain flour, for dusting

150g rough puff pastry scraps (see *Quick
    Tip* on page 218) or use ready-made
    puff pastry

I would strongly encourage you to make this, as it works really well as a starter or as a sharing dish on a dinner table surrounded by other accompanying dishes. This is a brilliant way of using up pastry scraps from the dauphinoise pie (see page 216), or alternatively, use shop-bought pastry.

Preheat the oven to 180°C fan/200°C/gas mark 6.

Heat the pan over a medium-high heat until hot. Place the onion halves, cut-side down, into the hot dry pan – do this in batches to get colour on the onions. They will also shrink down slightly so you will be able to fit more onions in than you think. Once all the onions have a nice colour, about 10–12 minutes, remove the pan from the heat and transfer the onion halves to a plate.

Sprinkle the sugar evenly over the bottom of the pan. Add the onions back into the pan, cut-side down, and cook over a medium heat until the onions sizzle and the sugar has caramelized. Arrange the onions so they look nice as you'll be flipping this over once baked, and make sure they are snug, too, with no big gaps. Put the thyme sprigs into some of the gaps, then sprinkle over the salt and drizzle over the sherry vinegar. Turn the heat down to low and cook for 5 minutes.

On a lightly floured surface, roll out the pastry to a 20cm (8in) round. Take the pan off the heat, then place the pastry carefully over the onions, tucking it down over the edges of the onions inside the pan. Poke a hole in the middle of the pastry with the tip of a sharp knife.

Bake for 30 minutes or until the pastry is golden and puffy and the onions have started to caramelize under the pastry. You should see nice bits of caramel coming through.

Remove from the oven and let it sit for 3–5 minutes, then carefully but quickly flip the tatin onto a large plate.

Serve warm with a sharp salad and/or a dollop of crème fraîche.

Quick Tip

If you're nervous about the tatin sticking to the pan when you flip it out, here is a little trick: once the sugar is caramelized, carefully pour out the caramel into a heatproof bowl, then line the bottom of the pan with a cut-to-size circle of baking paper. Pour the caramel back into the pan and reheat it slightly before adding the onions. Remember to peel off the paper before serving.

CHICKEN AND MARMITE PIE

SERVES 6

Equipment

flat baking tray; 26cm (10½in) round casserole/ovenproof pie dish, 5cm (2in) deep

For the pastry

400g strong white flour, plus extra for dusting

8g/1½ tsp fine salt

1 tsp caster sugar

300g cold unsalted butter, cubed

130ml ice-cold water

1 egg, beaten, for the egg wash

For the chicken filling

1 carrot, cut in half

1 celery stick, cut in half

1 shallot, cut in half

1 garlic bulb, cut in half

1 bay leaf

bunch of parsley stalks

1kg chicken thighs, bone-in, skin removed

1 litre water

100g unsalted butter

100g plain flour

100g crème fraîche

½ tbsp Dijon mustard

2 tbsp finely chopped parsley

1 tbsp Marmite (yeast extract)

bunch of spring onions, finely chopped

sea salt and freshly ground black pepper

Invite your friends round, ask one of them to pick up some chips from the local chippy en route and then present this pie on the table, served with the freshly fried chips and seasonal greens. There's something comforting and naughty about eating this way, making an effort in the most relaxed way, showing you care and eating chip shop chips at the same time – my type of night in.

First, make the pastry. In a large bowl or the bowl of a stand mixer or food processor, mix together the flour, salt and sugar. Add in the cold cubed butter and mix to form breadcrumbs either with your fingertips, the paddle attachment or pulsed. Pour in the ice-cold water and mix briefly and quickly into a dough. Tip this dough out onto a piece of baking paper and use the paper to bring it together as it's sometimes a touch sticky. Wrap the dough in clingfilm or a fresh sheet of baking paper and flatten it into a disc, then chill in the fridge for 2 hours or until firm.

Meanwhile, make the chicken filling. Preheat the oven to 180°C fan/200°C/gas mark 6.

Take a large saucepan, add the carrot, celery, shallot, garlic, bay and parsley stalks, followed by the chicken thighs and water. Season with salt and pepper. Bring to the boil and then turn the heat down to a gentle simmer. Skim off any white scum from the top and simmer for 30–40 minutes or until the chicken is tender (check it with a sharp knife). When the chicken is ready, remove it from the liquid and set aside to cool on a plate, then remove the chicken from the bones (discard the bones) and break the meat up into bite-sized pieces.

Strain the stock, reserving the clear stock as you'll use this. Discard the veg, garlic and herbs.

In another pan, make a roux by melting the butter over a medium heat, then add the flour and whisk well. Cook this over a low heat for 3–4 minutes until it turns to a light blonde colour. Gradually whisk in the stock (you should have approx. 700ml), making sure you carefully knock out any lumps. Allow this to come to a simmer, stirring, then once thickened, add the crème fraîche, mustard, chopped parsley and chicken. Add the Marmite and spring onions and mix well, then check the seasoning and adjust if necessary. The chicken pie filling is now ready to use.

Continued overleaf →

CHICKEN AND MARMITE PIE *continued*

To get ahead, make the filling the day before and refrigerate in an airtight container overnight. It will keep for up to 3 days like this. Use from chilled and add another 20 minutes on to the cooking time.

To assemble the pie, lightly dust your work surface with flour. Gently knead the pastry dough, then roll out to approx 5–6mm (¼in) thickness so that it's a larger round than the casserole/pie dish you wish to use. Slide the pastry round onto the baking tray and chill in the fridge for 20 minutes.

Preheat the oven to 180°C fan/200°C/gas mark 6.

Fill the casserole/pie dish with the prepared chicken filling – ideally it shouldn't be piping hot otherwise it will melt a layer of the pastry. Drape the chilled round of pastry over the dish and tuck the excess pastry down into the dish around the sides. Pinch the pastry every 1–2cm (½–¾in) around the edge to form an attractive finish (this also helps to secure the filling). Brush all over the pastry with the egg wash. Poke a hole in the middle of the pastry lid with the tip of a sharp knife.

Bake for 45 minutes or until golden brown all over and the filling is bubbling up a little through the middle.

Serve the pie hot with chips from the chippy (if you're like me) or mash and some seasonal greens or peas.

'There's something comforting and naughty about eating this way.'

BLINTZES

Continued overleaf →

MAKES 6

Equipment
large frying pan
(approx. 26cm/10½in diameter)

For the crêpes (makes 6 crêpes)
150g plain flour
pinch of Maldon or flaky salt
15g/1 tbsp caster sugar
2 eggs
250ml full-fat milk
50ml double cream
6 tsp unsalted butter

For the cream cheese and asparagus filling
(enough for 6 crêpes)
90g cream cheese
6 strips of Parma ham
12–18 asparagus spears, trimmed,
   blanched and cooled
6 tsp salted butter
freshly ground black pepper

For the cream cheese and caviar filling (enough for 6 crêpes)
90g cream cheese
6 tsp lumpfish caviar
1 small red onion, finely chopped
juice of 1–2 lemons
6 tsp salted butter
freshly ground black pepper

My husband's grandad, Lionel (Poppa), speaks lovingly about blintzes and how he grew up eating them. It spurred me to make these with Mattie's input, of course, and when I took my first bite, I sort of melted. You know? I had already eaten dinner by this point, but I couldn't help myself. I stood by the sink, hunched over, devouring them.

These would make an excellent brunch or even a fantastic starter at a dinner party, as the crêpes can be made in advance. They can be eaten solo, but I strongly urge you to give one of these fillings a go – the trick here is to gently fry the filled crêpes in salted butter.

Make the crêpes. In a large bowl, stir together the flour, salt and sugar with a whisk.

Crack the eggs into the middle of the bowl and add a splash of the milk. Start slowly whisking the mix, gradually adding the remaining milk as you whisk and knocking out the lumps, until you achieve a smooth batter. Finally, stir in the double cream, then leave the batter to sit at room temperature for 1 hour. Give it a quick stir just before use.

To cook the crêpes, heat the large frying pan over a medium heat, add 1 teaspoon of the unsalted butter and let it melt and sizzle. Add one ladleful of the batter and swirl it around the pan until it covers the base. Let this cook for 2–3 minutes or until the underneath is dry and the edges of the crêpe are starting to lift away from the pan edges. Flip the crêpe and fry on the other side for a few minutes until golden brown. Don't cook the crêpes until they're crispy, instead they should still have flexibility as you'll need to fold the filling inside later and they will get cooked again. Transfer the crêpe to a plate. Repeat with the remaining unsalted butter and batter to make six crêpes in total. Stack the crêpes on the plate, separating them with a sheet of baking paper between each one.

BLINTZES *continued*

Choose which filling you are using.

For the cream cheese and asparagus filling, take each crêpe and spread some cream cheese in the middle of it. Place a strip of Parma ham on top, followed by 2–3 spears of cooked asparagus. Season with black pepper. Fold each blintz by folding the bottom half up to the middle, then folding the two sides over and rolling it onto itself to close it. Melt 1 teaspoon of the salted butter in a frying pan over a low heat, then fry each blintz for a few minutes on each side until very slightly golden and warmed through (see *Quick Tip*). Serve warm.

For the cream cheese and caviar filling, take each crêpe and spread some cream cheese over half of it. Spread a teaspoon of caviar on the cream cheese, then scatter over some chopped onion. Season with black pepper and a squeeze or two of lemon juice. Fold each blintz by folding the bottom half up to the middle, then folding the two sides over and rolling it onto itself to close it. Melt 1 teaspoon of the salted butter in a frying pan over a low heat, then fry each blintz for a few minutes on each side until very slightly golden and warmed through (see *Quick Tip*). Serve warm.

Quick Tip

Each blintz can be cooked individually, or you can cook two at a time (in which case, add 2 teaspoons of salted butter per pair), taking care not to be tempted to whack the heat up, as these need to be fried slowly and gently so they don't dry up and become too crisp.

POTATO PIE

Equipment

25cm (10in) round deep casserole dish;
sturdy rimmed baking tray

For the rough puff pastry

600g strong white flour, plus extra for
dusting

3g/½ tsp fine salt

400g cold unsalted butter, grated

250ml water

For the dauphinoise

1.2kg potatoes (use a variety that roasts
well, such as Maris Piper or King
Edward)

500ml double cream

400ml full-fat milk, plus 2 tbsp for the
egg wash

6 garlic cloves, crushed and briefly
chopped

2–3 large pinches of Maldon or flaky salt

2 large sprigs of rosemary

2 large sprigs of thyme

lots of cracked black pepper

60–80g comté cheese, rind removed and
sliced into 2mm slices

1 egg, for the egg wash

I started making this pie at a neighbourhood restaurant that I worked at. I
was hell-bent on hand-rolling the puff pastry exclusively for the restaurant and
demanded that I did so. This potato pie became a regular on the menu along with
a layered meat version of a pithivier. It's a real labour of love and one that you
should consider making for friends and family. I like it served with seasonal greens
in the winter and a sharp salad with pickled walnuts in the warmer months.

You'll need to start this the day before you wish to serve it, as the pastry needs
several stages of chilling and the dauphinoise requires overnight chilling.

Make the pastry. In a large bowl, or the bowl of a stand mixer fitted with the paddle
attachment, mix together the flour, salt and cold grated butter. Pour in the water and mix
briefly to form a dough. Tip it out onto a large sheet of baking paper, then briefly roll it
vertically so it's a bit bigger than an A4 sheet of paper. Using the paper to assist you, fold
the top third down and the bottom third up and over that. Wrap in clingfilm or baking
paper and refrigerate for 2 hours or until it is firm and no longer slightly sticky to touch.

Lightly dust your work surface with flour. Take the pastry out of the fridge, making sure
the open seam is lined up vertically and the top and bottom are open folds. Roll the
pastry out lengthways and vertically to the size of approx. two sheets of A4 paper joined
together (about 60cm/23½in total length). Make a double fold by folding the top quarter
down to the centre and the bottom quarter up to the centre before folding these two
pieces together to close it like you would a book, then turn this so that the seam is again
lined up vertically. Wrap in clingfilm or baking paper and refrigerate for a minimum of
2 hours or until firm. Repeat this step. Once rested, the pastry is then ready to use (keep
it chilled until you are ready to use it).

Meanwhile, make the dauphinoise. Peel the potatoes, then wash and dry them. Set aside.

In a large pan, add the cream, 400ml of the milk, the garlic, salt, rosemary and thyme and
warm over a low heat until gently steaming – keep an eye on it and stir from the bottom
frequently to prevent it catching. Remove from the heat and discard the herb stalks.

Use a mandolin or a sharp knife and thinly slice the potatoes (to about 2mm thickness),
trying to do this lengthways or a way that means you get as much surface area as
possible, as this will help in the layering process. Once sliced, do not wash them as you
need the starch to help bind them.

Add the sliced potatoes to the warm cream and milk mixture, then crack lots of black
pepper into the pan. Stir well and keep this going over a low-medium heat for approx.
7–10 minutes until the potatoes are slightly tender, not cooked but softened and coated
in the cream mixture – it should all be bubbling gently. Taste the potato mixture, adding
more black pepper, if desired, and more salt, too, if needed. The salt levels will decrease
as it bakes, so season generously.

Continued overleaf →

Meanwhile, preheat the oven to 180°C fan/200°C/gas mark 6. Take two large pieces of baking paper and roughly press them into the casserole dish – the paper will help you to remove the baked potatoes later, so bear this in mind.

Using a slotted spoon, layer up the potatoes in the lined casserole dish – this doesn't need to be really precise but it will help to get a good slice through later if the potatoes are layered nicely. After each layer, ladle in some of the warm cream mixture. Repeat until you have used up all the potatoes, then pour any remaining liquid over the potatoes. Put a lid on or cover with foil and bake for 45 minutes.

Reduce the oven temperature to 160°C fan/180°C/gas mark 4, then remove the lid/foil and bake for a further 20 minutes. The dauphinoise is ready when you insert a knife and it doesn't meet too much resistance and it feels soft but not mushy. Remove from the oven and allow to cool fully before covering with clingfilm and refrigerating overnight.

To assemble the pie, line the sturdy baking tray with baking paper (it's important to use a rimmed baking tray as some of the butter will spread onto the tray as the pie bakes).

Divide the pastry into two pieces, making one piece slightly larger than the other. Roll out the smaller piece to a 35cm (14in) round, and the larger piece to a 40cm (16in) round, then place the smaller round on the lined baking tray. Remove the baked potato dauphinoise from the fridge and carefully flip the potatoes onto the pastry round, placing them in the middle. The potatoes will have set into one piece, so they will be really easy to work with. The diameter of the potatoes will be approx. 25cm (10in), which will leave a border around the edges when placed in the middle. Top the potatoes with the cheese slices. Take the second (larger) round of pastry and lay this over the potatoes. Use your hands and fingertips to press and shape the pastry over the potatoes, pressing the pastry edges together to seal.

Quick Tips

Keep the scraps of pastry by laying them flat, side-by-side, on a piece of baking paper, then gently roll together to form a sheet and use this again. I use the scraps to make a Caramelized Onion Tatin (see page 207) which I urge you to do, too.

My friend Bhavin makes this pie, but as he doesn't like making pastry from scratch, he buys ready-made puff pastry and wraps the potatoes in that instead – this works very well if you are short on time or don't like making pastry.

Trim around the pastry edges using a sharp knife, leaving a 2.5cm (1in) border all around (keep any pastry offcuts to use another time – see *Quick Tips*). Use a fork to seal the edges of the pastry. If you wish, you can use your fingers to create the pinched scallop effect around the edge of the pie (as shown in the picture) before baking. Chill in the fridge for 30 minutes.

Preheat the oven to 200°C fan/220°C/gas mark 7. Beat the egg and the remaining 2 tablespoons of milk together for the egg wash, then brush this all over the pie. Use the tip of a sharp knife to make a small hole in the top of the pie.

Bake for 30 minutes, then reduce the oven temperature to 180°C fan/200°C/gas mark 6 and bake for a further 30 minutes until golden all over. The base should also be golden rather than pale – you can check this by gently lifting up one edge, if it's not quite ready, return to the oven for a little longer.

Remove from the oven and allow to cool for 20 minutes before serving in slices. This pie is brilliant served warm with a sharp salad, but it's also great cold.

Store leftovers in an airtight container in the fridge for up to 3 days. If reheating, place in a preheated oven at 160°C fan/180°C/gas mark 4 for about 20 minutes.

FENUGREEK PARATHAS

MAKES 5

Equipment

large, heavy-based frying pan

200g white or multigrain chapati flour, plus extra for dusting

1 tsp fine salt

1 small white onion, finely chopped

1–2 fresh green chillies, finely chopped (deseeded, if you prefer)

¼ tsp coriander seeds, crushed

¼ tsp ajwain seeds

30g chopped coriander

15g/1 tbsp chopped fresh fenugreek/ methi

2 tbsp melted ghee or neutral oil, plus extra to brush the parathas as you shape and cook them

150ml tepid water, plus a bit more if needed

100g natural yogurt, to serve

mango/chilli/lime pickle, to serve

My mum and Biji would make these on the weekends, sometimes using up leftover dhal instead of water to bind the dough. There's always a bit of a difference between each of their techniques and a quiet dispute between which ones are better.

In a large bowl, combine the flour, salt, onion, chillies, coriander seeds, ajwain seeds, chopped coriander and fenugreek/methi. Mix this together well.

Make a well in the centre and add the melted ghee/oil along with the tepid water.

Use one of your hands to bring the dough together, it should be slightly sticky but hold together, then knead it in the bowl for a few minutes. Cover with a damp tea towel and let this rest at room temperature for 1 hour.

Divide the rested dough into five equal portions. Dust a wooden board or your work surface with flour. For each paratha, roll out a ball of dough into a 15cm (6in) circle. Fold each side of the circle into the middle to make a square, brushing the folded edges with melted ghee/oil as you go. Flip this parcel over, then roll it out again to a 15cm (6in) circle and brush all over with melted ghee/oil. Repeat to make the remaining parathas.

Preheat the frying pan on the hob over a low-medium heat for 4–5 minutes or until hot.

Place each paratha into the hot pan (cook one at a time) and cook for 3–4 minutes on each side, until golden and crisp all over, turning and brushing the paratha with melted ghee/oil a couple of times as you cook it to get it to colour.

Once each paratha is cooked, serve it immediately with some yogurt, or stack the cooked parathas on a plate and serve them all together with the yogurt and the pickle of your choice alongside. I tend to cook and serve them as I go when I'm making them for family and friends.

Once made, the dough will keep (wrapped) overnight in the fridge. Alternatively, once cooked, the parathas will keep, tightly wrapped in foil, at room temperature for up to 2 days, ready to reheat before eating.

TWICE-BAKED FOCACCIA

Equipment
28 x 18 x 5cm (11 x 7 x 2in) baking tin

For part 1 (day 1, or 12–16 hours before part 2)
150g strong white flour
⅛ tsp easy-blend dried yeast
150ml tepid water

For part 2 (day 2, or 12–16 hours after part 1)
500g strong white flour
1 tsp easy-blend dried yeast
350ml tepid water

For part 3 (day 2)
15g/1 tbsp Maldon or flaky salt
50ml tepid water

For part 4 (the very last part of day 2)
60ml olive oil, plus extra for greasing

For part 5 (day 3)
60ml olive oil

Mattie is also a chef, and a very good one, so I'm grateful to have his input in my bakes. He often throws a curveball at me and sometimes it works, sometimes it doesn't.

During a dinner that we were both throwing together at the last minute, he encouraged me to flip my focaccia over towards the end of its bake to crisp the top and bottom evenly. When Mattie worked at Noble Rot in London, they would do this with their focaccia twice a day for each service and it was glorious, always so crisp, light and fluffy. The oil gets soaked in really nicely so you win on both sides and are met in the middle with this pillowy soft centre.

Ideally, for the best results, you will need to start this focaccia two days before it needs baking with the preparedness to understand that the folding, touch and feel of the dough are all part of the joy.

Day 1 (part 1)

First make a pre-ferment – this is a really simple and fantastic way of improving the flavour of a dough. I use the same method for the Vodka Flatbreads dough (see page 227). Don't be scared, it's really really easy to do.

Put the flour and yeast into a container that is approximately double the size of the amount of flour and stir well. Add in the tepid water and mix well using a spoon or your fingertips. Cover loosely and leave at room temperature for 12–16 hours. This is called a poolish. It should bubble and look active during this time and it will rise and deflate slightly; it should smell ripe like a banana rather than acidic when it's ready.

Day 2 (part 2)

This is where the bulk of the recipe is made. The technique I use means that the 'work' is spread out throughout the day, which makes it really good to do in between errands or your job.

Take a really large bowl or a large rectangular container. Using your hands, mix the flour and yeast together in the bowl/container. Add the tepid water to the poolish (from Day 1) and mix roughly, then pour this into the flour/yeast mixture and mix using your hands and fingertips to form a rough dough. Cover loosely and set aside for 30 minutes in a warm place.

Continued overleaf →

TWICE-BAKED FOCACCIA *continued*

Day 2 *(part 3 and part 4)*

Stir together the salt and tepid water (part 3) in a small bowl, then pour this over the rough dough. Use your hands to squelch this through the dough evenly – it might require a bit more effort to get it properly into the dough. Cover with a loose clean tea towel and set aside in a warm place for 1½–2 hours. During this time, the dough will relax nicely.

Wet your hands slightly, then fold the dough four times. Do this by dividing the dough into four 'edges'; this is a lot easier if it's in a rectangular container but it's also fine if it's in a round bowl. Pick up the underneath of one edge and pull it over to its opposite side, then repeat three more times until each edge has been lifted and pulled over to its opposite side. Cover loosely with the tea towel and rest for 2 hours, then repeat this folding, then rest again for another 2 hours. Repeat the folding, then pour over the olive oil (part 4), leaving it on top of the dough, cover and refrigerate overnight.

Day 3

Lightly grease and line the base and sides of the baking tin with baking paper (this will help you to flip the focaccia later).

Remove the dough from the fridge and scoop into the prepared baking tin, it should fall into one layer, then as it relaxes it will spread to the corners. Allow this to come to room temperature, then use your fingertips to press some dimples into the dough sporadically – bubbles should start to show on top and this is good, the more bubbles the better. Set aside while you preheat the oven.

Preheat the oven to 180°C fan/200°C/gas mark 6. Place a rack/shelf in the middle of the oven.

The dough should look really loose and almost jiggly at this point, so push down again to form more dimples. Pour the second batch of olive oil (part 5) evenly over the dough.

Bake for 30 minutes or until golden with a nice thin crust.

Remove from the oven, then leave the focaccia to sit for 5 minutes before carefully flipping it over in the tin. Return to the oven and bake for a further 15 minutes, until golden all over.

Remove from the oven and allow to cool slightly in the tin, then tip the focaccia out onto a wire rack to cool completely before slicing and eating.

This focaccia is best eaten on the day it is made. It can also be wrapped in clingfilm and frozen; defrost and warm through in a low oven to eat.

VODKA FLATBREADS

MAKES 6 X 15–20CM (6–8IN)
FLATBREADS

Equipment
large baking tray; 15–20cm (6–8in) heavy-based frying pan or cast iron skillet

For the poolish
150ml tepid water
150g strong white flour
¼ tsp easy-blend dried yeast

For the dough
320g strong white flour
9g/1¾ tsp Maldon or flaky salt
¼ tsp easy-blend dried yeast
110ml tepid water
olive oil, for greasing and drizzling

For the vodka sauce
generous glug of olive oil, plus extra for cooking the flatbreads
1 small onion, diced
4 garlic cloves, roughly chopped
½ tsp chilli flakes
50g tomato purée
1 x 400g can chopped tomatoes
50ml double cream
20ml vodka
sea salt and freshly ground black pepper

To finish the flatbreads
100g firm/block mozzarella cheese, roughly chopped
small handful of basil, leaves picked
extra virgin olive oil, for drizzling

When I visited New York for the first time, I kept seeing penne alla vodka and pizza alla vodka on the menu. I managed to eat penne alla vodka once out there, but each time I went to order the pizza version it had sold out. I couldn't stop thinking about it when I returned home, so I decided to create and test a version for you. My flatbread dough works a treat and I've been using it for years at various pop-ups. Feel free to top the flatbreads with whatever you choose. The vodka sauce can also be made separately and used for pasta – it's very good.

For this dough, I start by making a poolish, which is a pre-ferment, and this will improve the flavour of the dough without using a sourdough starter. You'll need to start this recipe a couple of days before you want to cook and eat the flatbreads.

Day 1

Make the poolish by stirring together the water, flour and yeast in a large container. Cover and leave at room temperature overnight.

Day 2

Make the dough. In the bowl of a stand mixer using the dough hook, mix together the flour, salt and yeast, then add in the water and all of the poolish. Mix on a low-medium speed until a dough forms. Turn the machine off and let it relax for 5 minutes, then mix on a medium speed for 10–15 minutes until a smooth dough forms.

Generously grease a large bowl with olive oil. Shape the dough into a ball and place in the bowl, drizzle a little olive oil over the top, then cover and leave at room temperature for 6 hours.

Evenly portion and roll the dough into six balls, then dip each one in olive oil to coat and place on the baking tray. Cover loosely with clingfilm and refrigerate overnight.

Continued overleaf →

VODKA FLATBREADS *continued*

Day 3

The next day, first make the vodka sauce, then shape and cook the flatbreads.

For the vodka sauce, gently heat the generous glug of olive oil in a saucepan, then add the onion and stir over a medium heat until softened, about 6–7 minutes. Add the garlic and chilli flakes and cook for a few minutes, but do not let the garlic catch. Add the tomato purée and mix well over a medium heat. Season to taste with salt and pepper. Cook for a few more minutes before adding the canned tomatoes, then simmer, uncovered, for 15 minutes until it has thickened.

Use a stick blender to blitz the sauce (or transfer to a blender and blitz until smooth, then return to the pan). Add the cream and heat through, then add the vodka and cook over a high heat for a few minutes until the sauce is smooth and bubbling. Turn off the heat and allow to cool before using on the flatbreads.

Take the dough balls out of the fridge 20 minutes before using. If you have a home pizza oven, use that to cook the flatbreads (following the manufacturer's instructions), if not, use the frying pan/grill method as follows.

Using your hands, stretch each portion of dough out to a 15–20cm (6–8in) circle, depending on how thick you like your flatbreads.

Preheat the grill to high. Preheat the dry frying pan or skillet over a high heat until hot.

To cook each flatbread, drizzle a little olive oil into the hot frying pan/skillet. Gently lift a round of dough into the hot pan, then spoon over a portion of the vodka sauce and add some mozzarella on top, then let it cook for 2–3 minutes over a medium heat, until the top edges of the flatbread look dry. Put the pan/skillet under the grill and cook until the top is puffed, the edges are dark golden and the cheese is bubbling. Transfer to a serving plate, while you cook the rest in the same way.

Serve warm with basil leaves scattered over and a drizzle of extra virgin olive oil.

JALAPEÑO POPPER GOUGÈRES

MAKES ABOUT 30 CANAPÉ-SIZED GOUGÈRES

Try these the next time you need to make canapés or snacks for a get-together – they are delicious and will be very popular with your guests!

Equipment
large flat baking tray

1 x quantity of choux pastry (see page 39)
½ tsp smoked paprika
50g strong hard cheese like Parmesan, mature Cheddar or Gruyère cheese, finely grated, plus a little extra for serving
25g (drained weight) pickled jalapeños, drained and finely chopped
150g cream cheese
finely grated zest of ½ lemon and juice of 1 lemon
4 spring onions, finely chopped
sea salt and freshly ground black pepper

Make the choux pastry according to the instructions on page 39.

After the eggs have been added, stir in the smoked paprika and 25g of the grated hard cheese and mix well.

Preheat the oven to 190°C fan/210°C/gas mark 6½. Line the large baking tray with baking paper.

Spoon the choux mixture into a piping bag fitted with a 1cm (½in) round nozzle. Pipe 2–3cm (¾–1¼in) rounds onto the lined baking tray, leaving enough room between each for them to grow (you'll make about 30).

Bake for 18 minutes, then reduce the oven temperature to 170°C fan/190°C/gas mark 5 and bake for a further 5–8 minutes or until hollow and crisp – they should easily lift off the paper when they are ready.

Remove from the oven. Take a round piping nozzle and use the tip of the nozzle to create a hole in the base of each choux bun – this will be used as the point of entry to pipe the filling in later and doing this now helps to release excess steam. Transfer to a wire rack and cool completely.

Make the filling by mixing together the pickled jalapeños, cream cheese, the remaining 25g of the grated hard cheese, the lemon zest and juice and spring onions in a bowl. Season with salt and pepper.

Spoon the filling into a piping bag fitting with a 1cm (½in) round nozzle. Fill each choux bun with the filling by inserting the nozzle into the bottom of each one and pressing on the bag. Once each choux bun is filled, place it bottom-side down onto a serving plate.

Sprinkle a little extra finely grated cheese over the gougères and serve immediately.

The filling can be made and kept in an airtight container in the fridge for up to 2 days, but the gougères are best served as soon as they are filled.

SAMOSAS

MAKES 28

Equipment

large frying pan; a couple of flat baking trays; deep-fat fryer, or large, deep, heavy-based saucepan

For the filling

1.2kg whole potatoes in their skins

80ml neutral oil, such as sunflower, vegetable or rapeseed oil

2 tsp jeera/cumin seeds

2 large onions, finely chopped

3–5 fresh green chillies, finely chopped with the seeds (add to suit your taste)

250g frozen (or shelled fresh) peas

4 tsp fine salt

1 tsp ground cumin

1 tsp ground coriander

2 tsp garam masala

½ tsp amchoor (green mango powder)

30–40g finely chopped coriander

For the pastry

500g plain flour

¼ tsp ajwain seeds (optional)

1½ tsp fine salt

5–6 tbsp neutral oil, such as sunflower, vegetable or rapeseed oil, plus extra for greasing

approx. 350ml warm (tepid) water

For the 'glue'

100g plain flour

60ml water

approx. 1.5 litres vegetable or sunflower oil, for deep-frying

When I was growing up, I spent many afternoons sitting at a dining table covered in newspaper, assembling rows and rows of samosas – but assembling only and not making the filling, as I was only allowed to do the filling much later on with my mum's strict guidance. We were getting the samosas ready for a family gathering or, better still, stockpiling them for the freezer so we could eat them freshly fried after school.

Getting a recipe out of my mum is hard work; a direct quote from her and a bit of advice during our time together writing this was, "People have to use their common sense."

Make the filling. Steam the potatoes in their skins over a pan of boiling water for about 30 minutes or until tender, then cool, peel and chop into 1cm (½in) dice.

Heat the oil in a large saucepan, then add the jeera/cumin seeds and fry over a medium heat for a minute, then add the onions and fry for a few minutes, stirring frequently. Add the green chillies and stir well, then add the potatoes, peas, salt and ground spices and stir well. Turn the heat off, stir through the chopped coriander and then taste the mixture, adjusting the seasoning with a little extra salt, if needed. Leave to cool at room temperature before using.

Meanwhile, make the pastry. In a large bowl, combine the flour, ajwain seeds (if using) and salt, stirring together well. Create a well in the middle, then add the oil and warm water and use one hand to bring it together into a rough dough. It should be slightly damp and not dry, so if you need to add another splash of water, do so. The dough now needs to rest for 1 hour at room temperature, covered with a damp tea towel.

To prepare the samosa pastry for filling, divide the dough into 14 equal portions. Preheat the large frying pan on the hob so it's at a medium-low heat.

On a lightly oiled workbench, roll out each portion of dough to a round, approx. 20–23cm (8–9in) in diameter and approx. 2–3mm (1/16–⅛in) thick (it should be thin).

Use your fingertips to put each round into the hot frying pan just for a few seconds on each side, turning once. The aim isn't to gain colour but instead to seal the pastry briefly. Transfer to a plate and cover with a clean damp tea towel. Repeat with each round of dough, one at a time, stacking them up under the tea towel until you've sealed all of them.

Continued overleaf →

SAMOSAS *continued*

Now to fill your samosas. Get your workbench ready – my mum always lays down newspapers, then places a couple or so baking trays on top before assembling the samosas and I think this helps with the mess. Line the baking trays with baking paper. Make the 'glue' by mixing the flour and water together in a bowl.

Cut the sealed rounds of dough in half so you have 28 semi-circles in total. Using your hands, take one semi-circle, with the curved side facing towards you, then fold one third from one side across to create a triangle shape across the crescent, and brush this side with the 'glue'. Bring the other side over and use your fingers to seal the edges. This will create a triangular pocket. Fill with some filling, leave a 1cm (½in) gap at the top. Brush a bit more 'glue' inside and use a fork to seal the samosa around the edge. Transfer the samosa to a lined baking tray and keep covered with the tea towel as you go. Repeat with each semi-circle of dough and the rest of the filling to make 28 samosas in total.

Heat the oil in the deep-fat fryer or large, deep, heavy-based saucepan over a medium-low heat until it's 160°C/320°F or until a cube of bread browns in about 45 seconds.

Add the samosas to the hot oil in batches of 3–4 and deep-fry gently for a few minutes on each side, turning once, until they are evenly golden all over and crisp (the filling should be piping hot once they are fried). Lift the cooked samosas out of the oil using a slotted spoon or the basket of the deep-fat fryer and drain on kitchen paper. Repeat with the remaining samosas, remembering to bring the oil back up to temperature before frying each batch.

Either keep the fried samosas warm in a low oven while you cook the rest, or serve them as you go, which is what I do. Cool the fried samosas for a few minutes before eating. These are best served with tamarind chutney, coriander chutney, or my childhood favourite – tomato ketchup.

The uncooked shaped and filled samosas will keep in an airtight container in the fridge for up to 3 days. Deep-fry them as above to serve. Or they can be frozen for up to 1 month – simply deep-fry from frozen, but add on a few more minutes frying time.

SODA BREAD

MAKES 1 LARGE LOAF;
SERVES 8–10

This is excellent for when you need a quick loaf of bread for the table. It's best eaten with lots of salted butter.

Equipment

flat baking tray

200g plain wholemeal flour, plus extra for dusting

150g strong white flour

50g dark rye flour

100g porridge/rolled oats , plus extra for sprinkling

300ml buttermilk

100ml water

150g black treacle

10g/2 tsp Maldon or flaky salt

10g/2 tsp bicarbonate of soda

5g/1 tsp baking powder

Preheat the oven to 200°C fan/220°C/gas mark 7. Line the baking tray with baking paper and liberally dust it with some extra wholemeal flour.

Place all your flours and the oats in a mixing bowl and whisk together.

In a separate large mixing bowl, mix together the buttermilk, water and black treacle until well combined, then add in the salt, bicarbonate of soda and baking powder and mix.

Make a well in the centre of the dry ingredients and pour in the wet mixture. Bring the mixture gently together until you have a dough. It's important not to overwork the mix here, otherwise you'll end up with a tough, stodgy bread.

Lightly shape the dough into a rough oval, about 3.5cm (1¼in) thick, and place on the flour-dusted baking tray. Dust the top of the loaf with wholemeal flour and a sprinkling of oats, then score the top with two or three slashes using a sharp knife.

Bake for 10 minutes, then turn the oven temperature down to 160°C fan/180°C/gas mark 4 and bake for a further 20 minutes or until risen and lightly browned – the loaf should lift off the paper with ease when it's ready.

Remove from the oven, transfer the loaf to a wire rack and leave to cool.

Slice the soda bread and serve with lots of salted butter.

Soda bread is best eaten fresh on the day it's made, but it can be enjoyed toasted for a couple of days after. It also freezes well – wrap in clingfilm, or pre-slice and transfer to a freezer bag, freeze for up to 1 month, then defrost at room temperature before serving.

LANCASHIRE CHEESE AND GREEN CHILLI TART

SERVES 6–8

Equipment

20cm (8in) loose-based round tart tin; sturdy flat baking tray

For the pastry

125g plain flour, plus extra for dusting

45g cornflour

pinch of fine salt

100g cold unsalted butter, cubed

1 egg yolk

2 tbsp cold full-fat milk

1 egg, beaten, for the egg wash

For the filling

30g unsalted butter

2 large onions, finely sliced

½ tsp Maldon or flaky salt, plus an extra pinch

1 tsp ground white pepper, plus an extra pinch

3 tbsp water

300ml double cream

4 egg yolks

100g Lancashire cheese, grated

2 fresh Thai green chillies, finely chopped (deseeded, if you prefer)

This savoury tart works nicely served with a sharp salad in the autumn – the cheese and chilli both bringing comfort and warmth.

To make the pastry, in a stand mixer fitted with the paddle attachment, or a food processor, or in a large bowl, combine the flour, cornflour and salt. Mix well.

Add in the cold cubed butter and mix/pulse until the butter disappears and you have the texture of crumbs. If doing this by hand, rub into crumbs with your fingertips.

Beat the egg yolk and milk together in a small bowl, then add to the crumbed mixture and mix quickly to form a dough. Don't overwork the mixture, just bring it together until you have an evenly smooth dough. Flatten into a disc, wrap in clingfilm and chill in the fridge for 1 hour or until firm. Or freeze it at this stage for up to 3 months (defrost before use).

While the pastry is resting, cook the onions for the filling. Melt the butter in a medium saucepan, then add the onions and cook over a medium-low heat for 3–4 minutes. Add the salt and white pepper, cover with a lid and cook the onions very gently for 10 minutes until soft and translucent (don't allow them to colour), then add the water and cook, uncovered, for a further 20 minutes until the water has evaporated and the onions are soft and sweet. Remove from the heat, then spread the onions out on a tray/plate and leave to cool.

Preheat the oven to 160°C fan/180°C/gas mark 4. Place the sturdy baking tray on a shelf/rack in the centre of the oven to preheat.

Remove the pastry from the fridge and let it soften for 10 minutes or so. Lightly dust your work surface with flour, then roll out the pastry to a round with a thickness of 5mm (¼in) and use it to line the tart tin, leaving a slight overhang of pastry.

Continued overleaf →

Blind-bake the pastry. Prick the bottom of the pastry case all over with a fork, then line the pastry case with a sheet of baking paper and fill to the top with baking beans or dried rice/lentils. Put this on the preheated baking tray in the oven and bake for 25 minutes or until golden on the edges and dry to touch. Carefully remove the baking paper and beans, then return to the oven (on the baking tray) for 10 minutes, until the base is golden. Remove from the oven and brush the pastry base with the egg wash, then return to the oven for a further 5 minutes. Remove from the oven and set aside for 10 minutes.

Finish the filling. Mix the cream, egg yolks, cooled onions, the cheese and green chillies together in a bowl until combined. Add an extra pinch each of salt and white pepper. Pour this mixture into the blind-baked tart case.

Bake (on the baking tray) for 30–40 minutes until the filling is set and golden.

Remove from the oven and cool slightly in the tin (on the baking tray), then use a small serrated knife to tidy up the edges of the tart and cut off any excess pastry.

Carefully remove the tart from the tin and place it on a serving plate/board. Serve warm with a mustardy watercress salad.

This tart can also be enjoyed cold. Leftovers will keep in an airtight container in the fridge for up to 2 days, but the pastry will soften.

'The cheese and chilli both bringing comfort and warmth.'

'NDUJA SAUSAGE ROLLS

MAKES 20

Equipment
small flat baking tray; large flat baking tray

1.2kg sausage meat (flavour of your choice – see *Quick Tips*)

1 egg, beaten with a pinch of fine salt, for the egg wash

For the 'nduja butter
350g unsalted butter, softened

80g 'nduja

1 tbsp plain flour

finely grated zest of 1 lemon

For the pastry
500g strong white flour, plus extra for dusting

5g/1 tsp fine salt

100g cold unsalted butter, cubed

250ml water

juice of ½ lemon

I'm upping my pastry game here a little by making a 'nduja butter that I then use as a butter block to fold into the dough to create perhaps the best sausage rolls you've ever tasted.

The pastry needs several chilling stages, so it's best to make the pastry the day before you want to shape and bake the sausage rolls. It keeps refrigerated for up to 3 days and it also freezes well for up to 1 month (defrost overnight in the fridge before use).

Prepare the 'nduja butter. In a stand mixer fitted with the paddle attachment, or in a bowl using a wooden spoon, beat the butter and 'nduja together until homogeneous, then add in the flour and lemon zest and beat well.

Scoop the butter out onto a sheet of baking paper, spread it roughly to the size of an A5 sheet of paper, then cover with the paper, place on the small baking tray and refrigerate until firm.

Meanwhile, prepare the pastry. In a stand mixer fitted with the paddle attachment, mix together the flour, salt and cold cubed butter. Mix well until the butter disappears. Add in the water and lemon juice and mix until a dough forms. This can also be done by hand in a large bowl – simply use your fingertips to breadcrumb the butter into the flour and salt before mixing in the water and lemon juice to form a rough dough. Tip the dough out onto a sheet of baking paper, then flatten and shape roughly into the size of an A4 sheet of paper. Place on a tray and chill in the fridge for at least 2 hours or until firm.

To fold the dough, I use the same method as for puff pastry and laminate the butter in, folding it once and then completing two double turns. To start the folding process, take the dough out of the fridge and dust the workbench with flour.

With a short side nearest to you, gently roll out the dough vertically until it's only slightly longer than a sheet of A4 paper. Next, roll the 'nduja butter a little on its own through the paper – this will help it to become a bit more pliable when worked into the dough. The butter shouldn't be rock hard, if it is, let it sit at room temperature for 20 minutes.

Put the butter on the dough so it fits roughly over two-thirds of the bottom of the dough. Fold the top third of the dough down over part of the butter and then fold the bottom third (with the rest of the butter on it) up over the first fold. Turn the dough 90 degrees to the right. This is called a single turn.

Roll the dough vertically to the same size as before, then repeat the above by folding the top third down and the bottom third up and over the first third, then turn by 90 degrees. Cover and rest in the fridge for 2 hours.

Continued overleaf →

Take the dough out of the fridge. Roll the dough out vertically as before, but this time it will need to be double the length to complete a double turn as you need more space. Do this by folding the top quarter down to the centre and the bottom quarter up to the centre before folding these two pieces together to close it like you would a book, then turn it 90 degrees, cover and rest in the fridge for 2 hours. Repeat the double turn and then cover and rest in the fridge for another 2 hours. The pastry is now ready to use – keep it chilled (overnight is fine) until you are ready to use it. It keeps refrigerated for up to 3 days and it also freezes well for up to 1 month (defrost overnight in the fridge before use).

Line a large tray with baking paper. Roll out the pastry to a rectangle measuring 56 x 46cm (22 x 18in), then cut it in half widthways so you have two 28 x 46cm (11 x 18in) pieces of pastry. Transfer these two sheets of pastry to the lined tray and place in the fridge for 20 minutes.

Remove from the fridge and place one piece of pastry on your work surface at a time. Cut each of the two pastry sheets in half lengthways so you have four 28 x 23cm (11 x 9in) strips. Leaving a 2.5cm (1in) border all around the edge, pipe the sausage meat down one of the longer edges of each pastry strip. Brush the outer edges with water, then fold one side of the pastry over the sausage meat to seal it. Use a fork to join the pastry together.Use your thumb to press and seal gently down the side. Repeat with the remaining pastry so you have four long sausage rolls. Transfer to the fridge for 1 hour.

Preheat the oven to 180°C fan/200°C/gas mark 6. Line the large baking tray with baking paper.

Remove the long sausage rolls from the fridge. Trim them to make them neater on the edge you have sealed them (see *Quick Tips*). Brush with the egg wash and cut each long sausage roll widthways into five equal-sized pieces to make your sausage rolls. Transfer to the lined baking tray.

Bake for 35 minutes, then reduce the oven temperature to 160°C fan/180°C/gas mark 4 and bake for a further 10–15 minutes until well-risen and golden – the underside should also be golden and not pale.

Remove from the oven and transfer the sausage rolls to a wire rack to cool before serving. Serve warm, preferably on the same day they are made.

Leftovers can be stored in an airtight container in the fridge for a couple of days and eaten cold or reheated in a hot oven.

Quick Tips

Use sausage meat of your choice (I use pork sausage meat and sometimes the type with caramelized red onion already in) and either buy it as a block of sausage meat or buy sausages, remove the skins and then pipe/roll the sausage meat as above.

Keep any scrap pastry and chill before re-rolling and filling to make a couple of extra rolls!

CONVERSION CHARTS

WEIGHT

METRIC	IMPERIAL
5g	⅛ oz
10g	¼ oz
15g	½ oz
25/30g	1 oz
35g	1 ¼ oz
40g	1 ½ oz
50g	1 ¾ oz
55g	2 oz
60g	2 ¼ oz
70g	2 ½ oz
85g	3 oz
90g	3 ¼ oz
100g	3 ½ oz
115g	4 oz
125g	4 ½ oz
140g	5 oz
150g	5 ½ oz
175g	6 oz
200g	7 oz
225g	8 oz
250g	9 oz
280g	9 ¾ oz
300g	10 ½ oz
325g	11 ½ oz

METRIC	IMPERIAL
350g	12 oz
375g	13 oz
400g	14 oz
450g	1 lb
500g	1 lb 2 oz
550g	1 lb 4 oz
600g	1 lb 5 oz
650g	1 lb 7 oz
700g	1 lb 9 oz
750g	1 lb 10 oz
800g	1 lb 12 oz
850g	1 lb 14 oz
900g	2 lb
950g	2 lb 2 oz
1kg	2 lb 4 oz
1.25kg	2 lb 12 oz
1.3kg	3 lb
1.5kg	3 lb 5 oz
1.6kg	3 lb 8 oz
1.8kg	4 lb
2kg	4 lb 8 oz
2.25kg	5 lb
2.5kg	5 lb 8 oz
2.7kg	6 lb
3kg	6 lb 8 oz

LIQUID VOLUME

METRIC	IMPERIAL
1.25 ml	¼ tsp
2.5 ml	½ tsp
5 ml	1 tsp
10 ml	2 tsp
15 ml	1 tbsp / 3 tsp
30 ml	2 tbsp
45 ml	3 tbsp
60 ml	4 tbsp
75 ml	5 tbsp
90 ml	6 tbsp
15 ml	½ fl oz
30 ml	1 fl oz
50 ml	2 fl oz
75 ml	2 ½ fl oz
100 ml	3 ½ fl oz
125 ml	4 fl oz
150 ml	5 fl oz
175 ml	6 fl oz
200 ml	7 fl oz
225 ml	8 fl oz

METRIC	IMPERIAL
250 ml	9 fl oz
300 ml	10 fl oz
350 ml	12 fl oz
400 ml	14 fl oz
425 ml	15 fl oz
450 ml	16 fl oz
500 ml	18 fl oz
600 ml	1 pint
700 ml	1 ¼ pints
850 ml	1 ½ pints
1 litre	1 ¾ pints
1.2 litres	2 pints
1.3 litres	2 ¼ pints
1.4 litres	2 ½ pints
1.5 litres	2 ¾ pints
1.7 litres	3 pints
2 litres	3 ½ pints
2.5 litres	4 ½ pints
2.8 litres	5 pints
3 litres	5 ¼ pints

LIQUID MEASURES

METRIC	IMPERIAL	SPOONS/CUPS
5 ml		1 tsp
15 ml		1 tbsp
30 ml	1 fl oz	6 tsp / 2 tbsp
60 ml	2 fl oz	¼ cup / 4 tbsp
90 ml	3 fl oz	6 tbsp
125 ml	4 fl oz	½ cup
150 ml	5 fl oz	⅔ cup
175 ml	6 fl oz	¾ cup
200 ml	7 fl oz	
225 ml	8 fl oz	1 cup
250 ml	9 fl oz	
300 ml	10 fl oz	1 ¼ cups
325 ml	11 fl oz	
350 ml	12 fl oz	1 ½ cups
375 ml	13 fl oz	
400 ml	14 fl oz	1 ¾ cups
425 ml	15 fl oz	
450 ml	16 fl oz	2 cups
(US : 1 pint = 16 fl oz)		
500 ml	18 fl oz	
575 ml	19 fl oz	
600 ml	1 pint	2 ½ cups
(UK: 1 pint = 20 fl oz)		
700 ml	1 ¼ pints	3 cups
900 ml	1 ½ pints	3 ½ cups
1 litre	1 ¾ pints	4 cups
1.2 litres	2 pints	5 cups
Or 1 quart		
1.5 litres	2 ¾ pints	

DRY VOLUME MEASURES

FOOD	IMPERIAL	SPOONS/CUPS
Biscuit crumbs	115g / 4 oz	1 cup
Breadcrumbs, dried	140g / 5 oz	1 cup
Breadcrumbs, fresh	55g / 2 oz	1 cup
Butter	25g / 1 oz	2 tbsp
	50g / 1 ¾ oz	2 tbsp
	115g / 4 oz	½ cup
	225g / 8 oz	1 cup
Cheese, cottage, cream, curd	225g / 8 oz	1 cup
Cheese, Cheddar, Parmesan, grated	115g /4 oz	1 cup
Cocoa powder	100g / 3 ½ oz	1 cup
Coconut, desiccated	90g / 3 ¼ oz	1 cup
Cornflour	140g / 5 oz	1 cup
Courgette, grated	200g / 7 oz	1 cup
Flour, plain	140g / 5 oz	1 cup
Flour, wholewheat	165g / 5 ¾ oz	1 cup
Mushrooms, sliced	55g / 2 oz	1 cup
Hazelnuts, peanuts	115g / 4 oz	1 cup
Oats, rolled	85g / 3 oz	1 cup
Olives, stone in	175g / 6 oz	1 cup
Onions, chopped	150g / 5 ½ oz	1 cup
Peas, frozen	115g / 4 oz	1 cup
Raisins, seedless	165g / 5 ¾ oz	1 cup
Long-grain uncooked rice	200g / 7 oz	1 cup
Short-grain uncooked rice	215g / 7 ½ oz	1 cup
Granulated sugar	200g / 7 oz	1 cup
Caster sugar	200g / 7 oz	1 cup
Icing sugar	115g / 4 oz	1 cup
Soft brown sugar	200g / 7 oz	1 cup
Demerara sugar	200g / 7 oz	1 cup
Sultanas	175g / 6 oz	1 cup

TERMS AND TRANSLATIONS

UK TERMS	US TERMS
baking paper	*parchment paper*
bicarbonate of soda	*baking soda*
biscuit	*cookie*
biscuit	*cookie cutter*
black treacle	*blackstrap molasses*
caster	*superfine sugar*
clingfilm	*plastic wrap*
cooking apple	*baking apple*
coriander	*cilantro*
cornflour	*cornstarch*
demerara	*turbinado (or raw brown) sugar*
double	*heavy cream*
easy-blend dried yeast	*active dry yeast*
frying pan	*skillet*
grill	*broiler*
hob	*stove*
icing	*confectioners' sugar*
jam	*jelly/preserve*
jug	*pitcher*
kitchen paper	*paper towels*
mature	*sharp cheese*
mixed spice	*apple pie spice*
natural	*plain yogurt*
nozzle	*tip (for piping bag)*
piping	*pastry bag*
pitted	*stoned*
plain	*all-purpose flour*
polenta	*cornmeal*
porridge oats	*rolled oats*
self-raising	*rising flour*
sieve	*strainer*
soured cream	*sour cream*
spring onion	*scallion*
stoned	*pitted*
storecupboard	*pantry*
strong white flour	*white bread flour*
tea towel	*dish towel*
tomato purée	*tomato paste*

INDEX

ACKNOWLEDGEMENTS

I found this book the most challenging and yet the most freeing one I've written yet. It allowed me to enjoy the comforts of baking at home and to properly organise my kitchen to make it functional and useable. After so many years of baking and cooking in restaurants, it felt amazing to suddenly find time to make all the things I would dream of perfecting on my days off. Through it all, I must thank all the friends and family who assisted in the eating part of all the food testing I carried out – I couldn't have done it without you!

My husband Mattie, who has really held my hand through so much of this – he helps me beyond words and is always there with honest opinions, energy to run to the shops, providing reassurance, testing on his days off and, of course, washing up! This book is special to me because it's the one that's seen us through raising a cat, getting married and the first trimester of pregnancy! It's been an ever-so-present consistency and at the front of my mind throughout it all.

Thank you to Pavilion for believing in my vision and working with me on book three. To the wonderful team: Kiron Gill for her patience, Laura Russell for her creativity, Steph Milner – a real full circle to be reunited again, and Kom Patel for always keeping me in mind! Thanks for your belief Team Pavilion – it's been a joy as always.

I'd also like to thank my agent Ed Griffiths and my stylist Koulla Sergi who works tirelessly and is always pushing for the best! To Barrie, The White Company, Whistles, French Connection, Glassworks, Birkenstock, Rejina Pyo, Ganni, DHPR, ALLSAINTS, Loop Cashmere, Russell and Bromley, and Kitri.

Mike Tsang! I love working with you, your flexibility and willingness to get stuck in with a smile is everything – plus I love that you always have an appetite! Everyone on the shoot: Amy Lau for the amazing lunches and company, Alvin Engutsamy, Natalie Dormer, Cherlisa Engutsamy, Bhavin Ragha, and Anca Gratiozi.

Rachel Vere for being a fabulous prop stylist. Julia Aden for her calm energy and hard work on the food styling – she is a real talent! And Ellie Fleming and Lucy Turnbull for assisting.

Anne Sheasby, for meticulously going through this book with a fine comb, for working so hard to make this book as user friendly as possible and picking up on all the little details.

Finally, thank you dear reader – without you I wouldn't be on book three. Please get the pages dirty, scribble as much as you like and enjoy the pleasure of baking for yourself and others.

Lots of love x

Ravneet Gill is the author of the bestselling *A Pastry Chef's Guide* (2020) and *Sugar, I Love You* (2021). She studied at Le Cordon Bleu before taking over the pastry sections at St. JOHN, Llewelyn's and Wild by Tart. Now a freelance chef, she set up industry networking forum Countertalk in 2018 and online cookery school, Damson Jelly Academy.

Ravneet has been a judge on Channel 4's 'Junior Bake Off' alongside Liam Charles since 2020. She is also a judge on Channel 4 and Netflix show 'Five Star Kitchen' alongside Mike Reid and Michel Roux Jr. She has written for the *Telegraph* as a pastry specialist and is a regular columnist for *Guardian Feast*. Ravneet lives in London, UK, with her husband Mattie and her cat Armond. This is her third book.

First Published in the United Kingdom in 2023 by
Pavilion
An imprint of HarperCollinsPublishers Ltd
1 London Bridge Street
London SE1 9GF

www.harpercollins.co.uk

HarperCollinsPublishers
Macken House
39/40 Mayor Street Upper
Dublin 1
D01 C9W8
Ireland

10 9 8 7 6 5 4 3 2 1

First published in Great Britain by Pavilion
An imprint of HarperCollinsPublishers 2023

ISBN 978-0-00-860385-4

MIX
Paper | Supporting
responsible forestry
FSC™ C007454
FSC
www.fsc.org

This book is produced from independently certified FSC™ paper to ensure responsible forest management.
For more information visit: www.harpercollins.co.uk/green

Publishing Director: Stephanie Milner
Commissioning Editor: Kiron Gill
Editor: Anne Sheasby
Editorial Assistant: Shamar Gunning
Design Director: Laura Russell
Layout Designer: Kei Ishimaru
Production Controller: Grace O'Byrne
Photographer: Mike Tsang AKA @freshmikeeats
Food Stylist: Julia Aden
Prop Stylist: Rachel Vere
Indexer: Hilary Bird

Printed and bound in China by RR Donnelley APS